I0623365

GRACIOUS
QUOTIENT™

GRACIOUS QUOTIENT™

Evolving from Compassion to Graciousness

Karen Laszlo and Hollie Margrave

FIRST EDITION

ISBN: 979-8-9894740-0-4

DEDICATION

We dedicate this book and its work to the Divine.

CONTENTS

INTRODUCTION
Embarking on a Journey of Graciousness

Discovering the Gracious Quotient was a journey, an exploration of why we have a soul when we don't feel connected to it. With the plethora of our life experiences, both in joy and pain, what is the purpose of our experiences? How do we manage the impact of those experiences? How do we transcend the limitations of our minds?

We spent years studying various "ways of being" that exist within our culture, absorbing wisdom from spiritual retreats, collaborating with therapists, meditating, and seeking our own connection with the Divine. While these were helpful on a human level, nothing seemed to make us feel connected to our souls. The phrase, "we are all a collective"—connected to each other through our souls—didn't feel authentic, yet we wanted to explore this and understand what this really meant.

During our journey, we stumbled upon how human understanding of the soul has evolved. So, our focus turned toward meditating and listening to our souls. What we found was an unexpected enlightenment. Our minds were trying to interpret what we were discovering, and we needed to allow our souls to speak to us in a way that changed our perception—that changed the way we lived in this world and how we moved forward.

This discovery of what we now know as the "Gracious Quotient" has changed our lives and those with whom we have shared this work. Living in graciousness can help you move beyond compassion; to be more loving, kind, and generous to yourself without guilt and with a tenderness that opens your connection to the Divine, to others, and to your very humanness, and how you respond to this world and those who live in it.

We have been led to believe that compassion is the cornerstone of human connection and the Divine. Yet, during our journey, we uncovered that this didn't feel authentic. We uncovered that compassion, defined as "suffering together," might inadvertently rob individuals of dignity and respect due to its underpinning of judgment and pity. Compassion literally means "to suffer together." Among emotion researchers, compassion is defined as the feeling that arises when you are confronted with another's suffering and feel motivated to relieve that suffering. Must we suffer alongside others to extend a helping hand? What if you are not really required to feel the suffering of others? What would happen to those who suffer? Based on the theory of compassion, you need to feel their suffering, judge their situation, and identify what you think is better, or you will not do anything at all to help them.

These questions ushered us toward an uncharted territory—that the cornerstone of human connection and the Divine is not of compassion but rather of graciousness.

Graciousness, a state of kind and generous spirit, distinguishes itself from compassion, which can inadvertently strip away dignity and respect due to judgment and pity. Graciousness doesn't require judgment to feel motivation to offer support, love, or understanding to someone else. Compassion requires that you act, whether in words, deeds, or monetarily, based on what you are judging. Graciousness is freeing in that it is no longer relevant that you understand another, know what it feels like to be in their shoes, or have to stretch your imagination to secure an understanding of their situation. This paradigm shift is liberating; graciousness empowers both us and those we interact with.

Graciousness empowers us to be who we are while allowing others the same privilege.

Within the Gracious Quotient, there lies an essence that intertwines the Divine and the human through a thread known as the soul—where the Divine energy flows into the soul that then emanates out from the human body. This thread begins the moment of birth and never falters despite the twists and turns until it leaves our bodies and reunites with the Divine. That thread flows through the pages of this book, revealing the intricacies of our experiences, those moments of choice, questions that define us and the shadows (density) we navigate.

Our next phase of evolution involves embracing graciousness which comes out of pure love. Graciousness harmonizes with our soul, igniting the confidence to be our authentic self. Graciousness has many components; it is skill-based, harnessing the power of your soul, mind, and body, and is based on an evolutionary model that can propel us forward.

The Gracious Quotient isn't just a concept, it enables us to gauge our graciousness at any moment. Being in the higher levels of graciousness means that you are free to connect, experience, and trust, knowing that you see your own self and others in the purest way possible. It is a transformative journey where you don't take on anything that is not yours and authentically feel the full sense of your soul and the capability to be who you really are.

When you consider that graciousness is something that may be important to you, you will want to consider those things that interfere with the ability to be gracious. The journey to graciousness is about attaining skills, liberating ourselves from self-judgment, and fostering growth. It encourages us to tap into our soul, become sovereign, reframe our belief systems, and actualize our best selves.

Let's start with the levels of graciousness, and then we can move into the methods that will help you gain the skills to move up the scale to your true self more efficiently. What you'll discover is that there are ten levels of graciousness, and you can move up and down those levels all day long. You can move from a low level to a higher level or vice-versa. We'll share the levels in much more depth later in the book. For now, just know that you will start to self-identify where you fall at any given moment and gain the skills to move up the levels.

The 10 levels of the Gracious Quotient change daily or from moment to moment. You'll discover that the key is maintaining a balance where you stay within a high range of the Gracious Quotient. If you hit level 1 for an hour and then jump to level 7 for most of the day, that is awesome. As much as we want to see ourselves as being the most gracious, we must challenge ourselves to be honest and be temporarily "ok" with the lower levels of graciousness. It is the skills we gain and applying what we learn to become more gracious, that frees us from the judgment we place on ourselves.

We will also share the skills for becoming more gracious which include:

◊ Tapping into your soul and gaining the knowing/ intuition that is rightfully yours.

◊ Your right to be sovereign, to claim purity of intent, to create clarity, and respond from a place of graciousness.

◊ How to identify intentions that move your graciousness higher or lower and understanding that you have to be equally gracious to yourself and to others.

◊ Decide what your belief strands are, and which strands serve you in how you respond to situations.

◊ Using emotions as a teaching tool and not as an "I am" tool.

◊ Creating and actualizing what is in your best interest to keep you in a place of graciousness.

Our journey to understand this transformative concept is revealed through these pages. We invite you to explore the evolution of compassion into something more profound—into graciousness. This journey is not just about concepts; it's about experiencing life in a new light, embracing new perspectives, and resonating with your essence. The journey begins within—within our thoughts, within our actions, within our souls. It's a journey that challenges perceptions, transforms interactions, and invites us to embrace ourselves and others with unwavering grace. With each chapter, a new layer of understanding will unfold, offering insights that may transform the way you view the world around you.

It can be challenging to see yourself differently than you are used to; it starts with becoming aware of how you talk to yourself. How you speak to yourself is likely to be the same way that you project outward onto others. Is it possible to change the way you interpret situations and language to better communicate? As humans, we tend to make judgments on situations and others based on our beliefs or our surroundings. From this time on, take a moment to pause before speaking and before you let your mind take over your soul.

Being gracious to yourself is just as crucial as being gracious to others. Start with you before concentrating on anyone else.

You may want to read and re-read particular chapters, as there is valuable information for you to consider and practice. It is likely that in re-reading a chapter, you will find new information that you couldn't understand or even see the first time around. Often, our minds can only absorb so much information at once, and these concepts are likely very different from what you may be used to. You will also find that many of the chapters include a practice to integrate your newfound know-ledge, and you may find it helpful to keep a notepad and pen nearby to jot down any thoughts as you read.

Let's begin with how we define the key words used in this book.

We invite you to join us with this wonderfully gracious process.

Definitions

Attunement—Attunement is when an individual knowingly or unknowingly accepts the rules, beliefs, values and essence of a culture, family, or person. Your attunements, beliefs, intentions, and responses will change as you grow in your levels of Graciousness. Attunement is the first step in understanding how to become sovereign.

Authentic Self—Refers to the true and genuine version of oneself as opposed to the self that is shaped by societal expectations, cultural norms or personal insecurities. The authentic self is the inner most sense of self that is believed to be untouched by external factors. The authentic self is in full alignment with your soul and your soul's purpose. Being fully authentic can help to bring a sense of fulfillment and living in deeper connection with others.

Beliefs—Beliefs are convictions or acceptance that certain statements or claims are true whether there is evidence to support it. Beliefs develop from your core values. Beliefs shape your perspective, attitude and actions and are influenced by what you have become attuned to through culture, socialization, family and religion. Beliefs can change over time as you gain experience and knowledge.

Blessings—Blessings are gifts from the soul through your Divine connection. Blessings can refer to any positive gift given or received and easily occurs when a person is sovereign enough to allow their soul to do its work.

Chords—Chords are invisible links to others and works both towards a person and from a person to you and has an impact on both individuals. A chord between two individuals is a sharing of each other's current and will interrupt your ability to be sovereign. Imagine an invisible rope or chord coming from you to another and that attachment serves to tether you both together. Chords are an invasion of your sovereignty as they bind you to another and interfere with your ability to fulfill your purpose. Releasing these chords result in a positive impact for both individuals and serves to free you up for high impact soul work.

Compassion—Compassion is the emotional response to the suffering of others. Compassion requires that a person act, whether in feelings, words, actions or monetarily, based on what they are judging or told to judge, what they may pity, or what they feel is needed for another person, therefore compassion may disempower the individual you so desire to help. Compassion requires judgement: feeling for the other person, walking in the other person's shoes, or leaning into understanding what another person is going through in order to decide how you will offer support, love or understanding. Since compassion doesn't necessarily work in the way we intend it to, compassion may cause depression and bring harm to you and to others. Graciousness, on the other hand, empowers you and the intended person. By being Gracious, you offer acceptance to the intended individual without judgement, or pity.

Consciousness—An individual's ability to perceive their environment, thoughts, feelings, and emotions and their ability to process information, make decisions, and construct appropriate responses.

Core Values—A Core value is something you cherish the most, what guides your every move. It is the basic and most fundamental principles you live by and are guided by. Your core values were gathered from both what you were exposed to, and what you adopted, starting at a very young age. Core values can be seen in everything you think, feel, and do. Words a person may use to describe a core value may be: authentic, trustworthy, integrity, humble, independence, loving, kind, abundance, family, accountability, perseverance, discipline, etc. Core values are very personal. There are literally hundreds of words you can choose to define your core values.

Creation—The act of bringing something into existence using your soul and mind. It is in your best interest to create at the highest level of graciousness so that you attract the qualities of that level.

Density—Density refers to the intensity of emotions present in an individual's life. When emotions are high and thought patterns are deep the density is high and affects your soul's ability to express itself outwardly. Worry and fear dims the light of your soul as it is more about "what if "and lacks faith resulting in an individual moving into the lower levels of graciousness and into nebulous and ill will zones. This density then stunts an individual's ability to be self-aware and they are unable to fulfill their life's purpose. High density is like a million particles around you that you cannot see through and you then become fear based. Low density is like a few thousand particles where you can see clearly and accurately and can make the choice to move into higher levels of Graciousness.

Emotions— Emotions are associated with feelings, behaviors and thought that send out vibrations that others can pick up on. Emotions are a natural reaction and are triggered by a wide range of internal and external factors such as thoughts, memories, physical sensations, and social interactions. Emotions are brought to life by your intention which in turn, elicits your response to others or to a situation and are connected to what we have become attuned to from past experiences. Emotions alert you to your surroundings or what is happening to you. When emotions become more overwhelming, we call this high density, meaning you may not be able to see others or a situation clearly.

Energetic Current—The energetic current is the vibe that pulsates around us. It is the energy of the room, of others, or the combination of others energy that creates a current. An individual's energetic current can be read by others since this current pulsates. The pulse of the current can be high resulting in anxiety and distortion. Therefore, the goal is for the current to pulsate in a regulated flow allowing for higher levels of Graciousness. Emotions pulsate in different patterns and as an individual moves into lower levels of Graciousness, ie under level 4, they enter the nebulous zone where currents pulsate in an uneven pattern and cause havoc, pain and chaos. As you move to higher levels of Graciousness, your current naturally evens out to a steady pulse.

Essence—Essence is the intrinsic nature, a unique and indispensable quality that determines your character and becomes expressed in everything we do. Essence is the character of your soul. The Souls essence needs an open channel so that it can fulfill your life's purpose.

Gracious Shell—The gracious shell is the boundary

between your soul and your humanness. It is the outer parameter of your sacred soul and the inner parameter of your humanness. The shell protects your soul. The shell is not permeable however can contract and expand based on your level of Graciousness and the density that is around you. Therefore, it is critical that you remain sovereign to maintain the full expansion of your soul so that you can act with your souls purpose.

Graciousness—Graciousness is kindness and generosity of spirit and opens the path for who you truly are. Graciousness is the ability to be free of constraints, to express, and to expand all of who you truly are with certainty and intensity. Graciousness is the result of the purity of essence, knowing and pulse. It is a freeing concept, freeing you from judgement of self, of others, and more importantly opening you up to an acceptance of who you are and the blessings you are here to bring. Graciousness brings to you an acceptance of yourself, and of others, where there is no illusion of judgement and there is a deep acceptance for an individual just as they are and exactly where they are. Graciousness is the protector of the soul.

Intention—Intention is your mindset during an action. Emotions are enlivened by an intention resulting in a response to a person or situation. Intention is your hope, your aim, your purpose or your desire to satisfy.

Knowing—A knowing is the knowledge of the soul, your inner wisdom, your intuition. When pure, it is the whisper of the soul and comes from your Divine connection. Each of us has this knowing. A knowing is so deep and so pure that it surprises even us as it passes not from our minds but from deep within us so unencumbered, so smoothly, so eloquently, and so impactfully. It does not come from any education, it just is.

Mantra—A method used to free the mind from old thoughts that no longer serve you. A mantra is a phrase that is said over and over to protect and free the mind from distractions. Mantras can be sounds, words or sentences and used for different purposes to bring about a certain outcome. The repetition of a Mantra is believed to create a vibration that aligns with the energy of the Mantra and helps bring about the desired outcome.

Metacognition—Involves being aware of one's own cognitive process and being able to monitor, control and regulate them.

Moment of Choice—A moment of choice refers to a specific time when you are faced with a decision or choice to make. It can be significant or minor decision and is a point where you must choose and act upon it. In your moment of choice, what matters most is that you are at your highest level of graciousness–whether

15

that is a level 6, or even a 9. The moment of choice brings to the forefront all that you have chosen to be aligned with up to this point. It is so very important that in your moment of choice, you are making choices that are in the best interest of your soul—not your ego—and not for others, or for limiting beliefs. Remember, each moment of choice is yours and yours alone.

Nebulous—When an individual is exhausted and at times faces intense confusion combined with the lack of clarity as it relates to their soul, their emotions, their purpose, their motivations, and their values, they are nebulous.

Power—Individuals have power to make their own decisions and taking actions that shape their own lives and at times, the lives of others. It is not always positive and can be abused to harm or control others. Power is critical to manage your own life and if you hand your power over to others, you lose the space to fulfill your soul's purpose.

Pulse—The pulse is the frequency of your soul. A soft pulse represents an individual who can graciously receive, someone who is gentle, open, a strong listener and interpreter of what others say. A moderate pulse is the deliverer who has the unique opportunity and natural way of bringing others together. A rapid pulse is the giver who naturally find ways to give to others and feels an undeniable pull to do so. In each of these three pulses, when an individual is fully in alignment with their pulse, they will feel light and engaged with no expectation. Each pulse is required, and no pulse is more important than the other. While many of us have been taught that to give is Divine, understand this is not the case with the pulse. Each sector is Divine, critically important, equally important, and powerful.

Purity—Purity is when you are in highest alignment with your authentic self, your actions and there is no conflict within. You have no judgement, no preconceived notions, and you see all others and yourself as you truly are. Your goal is to unite with integrity, dignity and respect with sincere humility.

Self-involved vs Self-aware—Self-involved occurs when an individual is overly focused on themselves and their own interest and needs with little focus on showing interest, concern or caring for others. It is the darker side of the ego. The lighter side of the ego permits the individual to be aware of their own thoughts, emotions, and behavior and how they relate to the external world. A self-aware individual cares about others as well as themselves and understands their strengths, limitations and ability to reflect and shows high levels of metacognition.

Soul—The soul is an energetic form of knowing, filled

with knowledge of your past, present and future and comes from the Divine Source. The soul is incomprehensible to the human mind on how it actually works. In your physical body, your heart beats to keep the blood flowing which in turn keeps you alive. The essence of the human is the soul. The soul is separate from the physical form and is of the DNA of the Divine Source. Your intuition is whispers from your soul. The soul is made up of three parts: knowing, essence and pulse.

Soul Consciousness—The eternal, unchanging Divine piece of an individual that is separate from the ego, personality, emotions and the physical body. Connecting with soul consciousness enhances your connection to your unique intuition.

Soul's Purpose—The soul's purpose is the unique and specific reason or mission that your soul is here to achieve. It is the main reason a person is here for this lifetime. You can access your soul's purpose through appreciating the three elements of the soul: the knowing, the essence and the pulse. You can identify your soul's purpose with clear intention, purity and an openness for discovery.

Sovereignty—Sovereignty means that you have the right to govern yourself, the complete and utter authority and independence over you and your soul.

You have the right to remain just you, unto you, and you can decide what is within your best interest and your souls' best interest. Every person has a right to sovereignty and without accepting your sovereignty, you will give up your power to others thus creating chaos everywhere you go. Sovereignty is a requirement to fulfilling your soul's purpose.

PHASE I

Graciousness

CHAPTER ONE
The Invitation to Live a Gracious Life

Imagine a world where you can create the most beautiful life. Where you are free to be fully you and free to exist without harm to yourself or others. We invite you to create just that in the highest levels of graciousness. Welcome to the rest of your life.

This book was written for the express purpose of inviting you into your own life. Inviting you back into yourself, your soul, your true authentic self. You are invited to create the world you desire, the life you wish for, by tapping into the essence of who you are, your very essence, your intrinsic nature, and the undeniable quality of your soul that is of critical importance in this world. Because without your essence and ability to be gracious, you as an individual will create chaos everywhere you go. You will create disruption and perpetuate negative energy, as will others who are not gracious. Becoming gracious allows your soul to come through in all you do, the energy around you to settle and for you to become more peaceful. You will find your real, authentic essence in everything you do. This will create a shift in you that will be recognized as impactful, and you will begin to bring levity to tough situations, calm to crises, and peace to yourself.

So how does this feel?

Imagine the air swirling around you. The air feels fresh and pure as the gentle breeze creates a barrier, guarding you against forces aiming to take away your power, diminish your strength, erode your graciousness, and that seeks to limit the true essence of who you really are. Within this boundary, is a space of energy that is yours and yours alone, a sanctuary where your soul, your true self resides undisturbed.

This book is written so that you can create that space, discover your soul's essence, increase your "Gracious Quotient," and offer the blessing you were meant to be in this world. The blessing that you are, the "inner part" of you, your "true authentic self," your "soul," your "within," whatever you need to call it, is to be protected so that it can blossom and shine at all times.

Protecting Your Soul

The Gracious Quotient is a way to protect your soul, the best part of who you are. With graciousness, you are free to be you. Without graciousness, you will be managed or drained by others. In your true authentic essence, you are filled to the brim and beyond. You have firm boundaries, and within those, you can cherish, nourish, and activate all the blessings your soul is here to offer you and others. This creates the highest levels of graciousness for you and those around you, bringing into your world the many blessings that right-fully are a part of you.

Imagine that your soul boundary is a shell, with all the knowledge about you, with a life force so strong that you can't live without it. It is a beautiful force that expands and contracts throughout your life. When you lean into it, it guides and supports you with your best interest at its core. When life gets overwhelming, too demanding, or you are attuned to ways that are not in alignment with your soul, your energy starts to diminish. You lose your essence, your knowing, and your soul's pulse weakens. Without your true essence, you become deflated, even depressed. You go through this world not believing, not trusting, and living in the deepest, darkest fear. This lack of trust and faith, coupled with your fear, can close you in and stop any blessings you can offer, and this intensity of fear creates a swirl of a high-density barrier, like a dark gray cloud, preventing you from seeing and doing what you were born to do.

If you find this difficult to believe now, trust that by the end of this book, you will understand that you were born to bring blessings to yourself, others, and the world. Graciousness will support you in bringing these blessings to their fullness. With Graciousness, you can bump up against high-density emotions, fear, pain, humiliation, shame, anger, and destruction with suppleness—the ability to bend without breaking. With Graciousness, you can reduce this density and move freely, to ebb and flow with the world's energy, to be in your true essence.

How, then, do you bring in full graciousness and your full blessings for yourself and for others?

The Gracious Shell

The Gracious Shell is a boundary, a protective layer, that protects your soul and its blessings. Imagine this shell as a transparent outer layer three feet from your body above, below, and around you. You are in the center of this boundary. Your soul pulsates within this space with all the protection, love, connectedness, sovereignty, and positive power. The Gracious Shell protects everything within it, allowing your soul to expand, thrive, become empowered, and bring forth your blessings. Within this beautiful, safe space, you will find purpose, peace, contentment, and freedom from unwanted influences. Outside the shell exists all that tries to mold you and your responses, limiting what is rightfully yours to offer.

To help you understand this concept, imagine being in a grocery store and hearing some people laughing and others arguing. The laughter feels expansive, and the arguing feels contracting. As you get closer, you become immersed in the experience, and the density becomes thicker and limits your ability to see clearly. You may want to join in or intervene. You are in a high-density situation and have lost a sense of yourself, and you may want to intervene and ask the arguing couple to stop without knowing what their situation is. In a high level of graciousness, you accept the couple for who they are. Of course, if there is physical or emotional harm, you step in. Otherwise, you squeeze by and keep the density outside your impermeable high levels of graciousness. You continue your path without looking backward and fully accept those individuals as needing to express themselves in their own way. In the highest level of graciousness, you accept yourself as you are, in soul and humanness, and you accept others in the same way. The energy you share with others can be a blessing; it is all within your choice. Alternatively, you might find yourself experiencing feelings of sadness or empathy for them. In that instance, take a pause. Compassion has the potential to undermine our capacity to uphold our individuality, to stand firm, and to remain authentically true to ourselves. This is because compassion often entails making judgments, feeling sorry, and assuming a position of superiority—believing that one knows what's best. Graciousness, on the other hand, grants you the ability to navigate various situations with a gentle demeanor, a sense of calmness, and a genuine purity that safeguards against causing harm to others while preserving your own well-being. Graciousness is an embodiment of kindness, while compassion can sometimes verge on pity. Graciousness emanates an otherworldly quality, whereas compassion lacks thoughtfulness.

Life Purpose

As you think about your life's purpose, where you would like to grow, and how you would like to be rewarded, you will think about the ability for your mind to become settled, for your mind to trust your true authentic self. We encourage you to approach reading this book with the perspective that you hold inherent value and significance in this world. And that increasing your graciousness will increase your ability to do better, be better, and know better. Anger and hostility, pain and suffering are all part of being human, although some call it "karma" and others call it "deserving"— "You did this, so you get that."

Graciousness requires listening deeply to our true authentic self, our soul.

But how, then, do you explain children getting sick or a car wreck where a person is driving under the influence and crashes into you? Those situations where no one deserved to be hurt. How do you explain that? Some may say past-life karma or the wrong place at the wrong time. But rather than trying to explain these types of events, with graciousness, we recognize it just is. We are humans living in a human world, and we have experiences that we don't deserve or perceive as unfair. Again, we're judging what we don't deserve; the notion of deserving is irrelevant. What matters most is accepting that bad things can happen to the best of us. It's the human experience; this is life. Your true authentic self need not be compromised or impeded by these events. Despite enduring hardships, experiencing love, and aspirations for betterment, our authenticity remains intact when living a gracious life. So, as you accept the invitation to honor yourself, to live a life of graciousness, remember, the human experience is just that. We are human. We experience loss and joy, birth and death, poverty, and richness. While we may want to create meaning of this, perhaps consider the most authentic meaning in life is your true authentic self.

Space for the Authentic Self

As you read through the following chapters, we invite you to put yourself into a quiet space that allows you to remain open and not defensive, to consider who you really are, and invite yourself inward into this hidden knowledge that can now be truly yours. This hidden knowledge can be revealed so your true authentic nature can shine. Remember, being gracious is a process, not an event. If you choose graciousness, it will take time for you to learn and embrace a more evolved way of being.

Graciousness, however, goes beyond the mind and body and into the world of the soul. Graciousness requires you to become sovereign and strive to honor your soul, and free yourself from what others think—from external validation. Becoming familiar with your soul may seem difficult; however, the more you are determined to do so, the more your world opens up so you can fulfill the reason you are here. Of course, you will need time, patience, and a willingness to start filtering out old ways so that you can focus on your true authentic self.

Graciousness has the power to transform your belief system, reshape how you navigate emotions, and unlock the doorway for your soul's essence to emerge.

Being conscious of your Gracious Quotient will open the possibilities of releasing high-density emotions and energy and filling that space with what you were born to do. Even when you want more, want better, feel suffering and pain, lose loved ones, or go through a crisis, graciousness will help you remember that even in your humanness, you still have a soul that is pushing you to bring out your blessings to their fullest potential no matter how high the density the energy is around you.

Graciousness has many components: it is skill-based, harnessing both the power of the soul and your unique capabilities. The Gracious Quotient process will ask that you examine your entire life—your values and beliefs, attunements, and ability to be sovereign.[1] If you work toward graciousness, you will see a shift in how emotions are managed and will be able to allow the soul's essence to become strengthened, resilient, and shine through in almost any situation.

While you work through understanding and growing your Gracious Quotient, you will need patience. It can certainly be a challenge to see yourself in a different way than you are used to. Once you become aware of how you talk to yourself, you will begin to recognize that you may need to update what you are attuned to.[2] This attunement will assist you in comfortably transitioning into higher levels of graciousness. As you are learning about the Gracious Quotient, you may be tempted to focus on what others are doing and judge where they may fall on the levels. Remember to start with you before concentrating on anyone else. Keep in mind that if you speak to yourself in any given manner, it is likely you project those exact words outward toward others. As you change how you interpret situations and the language you use, you can better communicate, make fewer judgments on situations, and differ in your approach. Your attunements, beliefs, intentions, and responses will change as you grow in your levels of graciousness. You may take a moment to pause before speaking so that you speak from a higher level of graciousness.

Remember: Graciousness is a process, not an event; therefore, it will take time to learn, wholly embrace the concept and exist in Graciousness.

In Summary

We invite you to explore using graciousness as a way to get to know your soul, your true authentic self so that you can live a life of freedom from what others choose for you and what you are here to bring forth. The process we'll share begins by understanding what graciousness is, moving into the Gracious Quotient levels, and finally, how to become more gracious. Methods are offered along the way to become conscious of your Gracious Quotient and how to move it up a level or two by transforming your belief system and reshaping how you navigate the influence of others and emotions. You will notice that while these methods are easy to understand, it does take time to become more aware of when to use them. You will have many moments of choice. A moment of choice can replace confusion or the feeling of being stuck as you start to acknowledge what you are attuned to. This way, you get to decide how graciousness plays out in your life. We invite you to move toward patience, tenderness, and expansion of the beautiful life and the unlimited blessings that are rightfully yours!

CHAPTER TWO
What's in Your Gracious Shell?

Graciousness is the ability to be free, express, and expand oneself. In graciousness, we are offered Divine insight or wisdom that is bestowed upon us, a sacred knowing that becomes part of us that then can flow into the world as blessings, gifts that only you can bring to the world. This is why purity matters so much. In graciousness, you will have sovereignty and the space to be all of you, all you are meant to be, where you can bridge the gap between purpose and what your soul is permitted to contribute. And unbeknown to all others, you will have the respect of all the souls that exist since there is no difference between what you put out to the world and your soul's purpose. You will be free to walk in kindness without being taken advantage of, to walk in freedom and navigate life's journey, untethered from others' expectations, to be free to nourish yourself in the purest sense, much like sipping from the purest spring of water. Graciousness seems like an ethereal concept, while, in fact, graciousness preserves your ethereal quality. As stated in the last chapter, graciousness is kindness and generosity of spirit and opens the world for your soul to emerge. Many find graciousness a freeing concept, free from the judgment of self and others. Graciousness is also freeing in that it is no longer relevant that you understand others, know what it feels like to be in their shoes, or have to stretch your imagination to secure an understanding of their situation. Graciousness requires you to ACCEPT your soul and the souls of others. In graciousness, there is no illusion of judgment merely acceptance and respect for a person just as they are, exactly where they are.

Consider the Gracious Shell as a protective shell between your soul and your humanness. It is the outer perimeter of your sacred soul and the inner perimeter of your humanness. This shell can contract and expand based on your level of graciousness and the density around you. Therefore, it is critical that you are sovereign to maintain the full expansion of your soul so that you can act in your soulful purpose and bring forth your blessings.

Within the Gracious Shell

Within the Gracious Shell lies the truth of who you are, your soul's essence, your knowing, and the unique pulse felt by you and all those around you. The truth of who you are will unfold as you offer more space for graciousness to evolve. You must discover your soul's purpose on your own since others cannot do this for you. Your soul's essence is highlighted in everything you do, say, think, and act on. Each day, you express a knowing, a wisdom that you may not recognize as your own. There is a natural inclination to be surprised by that wisdom. When you were brought into this world, you came with your soul and the expectation you would learn how to care for your soul throughout your life and learn what is rightfully yours to offer and to protect. As a method of understanding, imagine you were also born with a soul's pulse that may be soft, moderate, or rapid. These pulses have deep meaning offering insight into the truth of you.

The truth of you unfolds over time though many of us wish to know this quickly so we can move on from discovery to actualizing.

Wouldn't it be grand if your parents were offered information about who you are from the moment of conception? Then, they could gently guide you to your soul. They could show you how to offer blessings to yourself and those around you. Perhaps, in the future, this will be an opportunity.

The truth of who you are lies within the Gracious Shell and can be discovered by seeking knowledge of your soul's essence, your knowing, and your soul's pulse. Below are a few concepts that are helpful to understand and relate to your soul's essence. You will find more profound insight and practices on the following in a later chapter.

Your Essence

Essence is the intrinsic nature, a unique and indispensable quality that determines your character and becomes expressed in everything you do. Your essence is pure, unchangeable, and your life's foundation. You can trust that no matter what, it will show up in everything you do for yourself, and for others, from your choices to your focus.

Essence is the character of your soul.

For example, you may naturally nurture others without thought, and when you examine your life, you find that everything you do has the essence of nurturing. No matter your career choice, nurturing is at its foundation. Or perhaps you find that since you were a small child, you sought harmony or worked to create harmony. Perhaps, when looking back, you see that others depended on you to bring harmony and balance. Take a look at your drawings or artwork, your relationships, your choices, and what came naturally. If math comes naturally to you, that is mental aptitude. Yet looking deeper, you may consider math as one expression of an essence of a builder, of seeing how to sequentially bring concepts together for a specific end result.

There are limitless essences and combinations of how we bring our essence into the world. The benefit of knowing and appreciating your essence is the freedom to be in alignment with who you really are and having the confidence to express yourself authentically. You enable your voice to be solid, to be heard, and to be real. Not being in your true essence is typically a result of high emotions, intentions not in alignment with your soul, and less purity around what you would like to see or achieve.

Knowing

A knowing is the knowledge of the soul, your inner wisdom, your intuition. When pure, it is the soul's whisper and comes from your Divine connection. We each have this knowledge and may recognize it when sharing it.

A knowing is the whisper of the soul.

A knowing is so deep and so pure that it is like a "whisper" not from our minds but from deep within us, so unencumbered, so smoothly, so eloquently, and so impactfully. It does not come from any education; it just is. When you have these knowing experiences, write them down for future reference and understanding.

Soul's Pulse

The pulse is the soul's frequency. Consider that there are soft, moderate, and rapid pulses of the soul. A soft pulse, or a receiver, represents an individual who can graciously receive, someone who is gentle, open, a strong listener, and an interpreter of what others say.

The receiver offers their blessings in such a way that naturally encourages others to offer their blessings. A moderate pulse, a deliverer, has a unique opportunity and natural way of bringing others together. With a rapid pulse, a giver naturally finds ways to give to others and feels an undeniable pull to do so.

A soul's pulse offers deep insight into your ability to receive, deliver or give.

When you identify your pulse type and fully align with it, you will feel light and engaged without expectation. Each type of pulse is required, and no soul's pulse is more important than the other. While many of us have been taught that to give is Divine, understand that this is not always the case. Each pulse is Divine, critically important, equally important, and powerful.

Practice: Unlocking Hidden Nature of your Soul

The following practice unlocks or finds the hidden nature of your soul, where you can begin to understand the essence of who you are, the knowing and the pulse of your soul. When you do this practice, you must first understand what your essence is and what your authentic self means. Your true authentic self is your soul and is void of your ego and all the attunements (beliefs, values, and rules you live by). The goal of this practice is to uncover the nature of your soul and give it the room to express itself.

1. Sit in a quiet space. And ask yourself, "Am I truly ready to attune to my soul?"

2. If you answer yes, grab a notepad or journal and a pen, and put on some beautiful music with no words or humming.

3. As you listen to this music, imagine yourself riding the waves of the music. And when you do this, imagine you're free of your body and mind. All there is is the expansion of who you truly are.

4. As you ride this vibrational wave, start to allow words to form, don't make sense of it. Just allow words to pop up. They could be simple as "cat" or "tree." Record or write down the words in your notepad or journal. Don't think about the words; just see them, or hear them.

5. Within a minute or two, those words will start to settle down, and you will start to feel an expansion in your chest, a freedom, a peace. This expansion is what you're trying to achieve. Your authentic self is now filling up more and more space.

6. If you can, just sit and ride the musical wave and hold that expansion in your chest and allow that to start integrating into your mind. Don't control it, don't ask it anything, just allow it to

swirl around your mind.

7. Allow the wave to permeate and remove other thoughts that will distract you, and ask for a sentence or a few words that you can string together. Maybe something like "a beautiful breath" or "the sun is shining."

8. After a minute or two, start to come back to your body and the room. Write down the few words strung together and allow those few words to sit with you throughout the day. This string of words was given to you by your soul so that you can start tapping into it throughout the day.

Think about the words you have received as you go through the day, and become aware of those words in everything you do. You may be writing a book, you may be giving a lecture, or you may be having to do finance. And when looking at it, remember the words, i.e. "The sun is shining through." As you do this type of practice over a series of weeks, months or even years, you'll start to uncover the hidden truth. The hidden nature of who you really are and what you are here to do.

In Summary

The Gracious Shell is the outer perimeter of the soul and the inner perimeter of your mind and body. It is the protective barrier of your essence, knowing, and pulse and it will take time to test out, settle with, acknowledge, and appreciate your Gracious Shell. It will take an equal amount of time to understand the blessings you bring to yourself and to those around you. You will begin to appreciate that your mind is not part of the soul and that your soul influences your mind in ways you have yet to discover. You need to use your mind to manage all the information and to figure out how to honor what is in the shell and how to keep your beliefs, values, intent, and emotions outside of this shell. While it is common to believe the mind, body, and spirit are essential to keep in balance, consider that the spirit is the most precious of the three and deserves the most room.

CHAPTER THREE
Evolving from Compassion to Graciousness

Graciousness is the ability to be released from constraints to express and expand all you truly are with certainty and intensity. Graciousness is a concept freeing you from the judgment of self and of others, and more importantly, that opens you to self-acceptance and the blessings you are here to bring. Graciousness is kindness and generosity of spirit where there is no illusion of judgment, and there is an acceptance for an individual just as they are and exactly where they are.

Remember, graciousness begins within the Gracious Shell and extends outward into the world. It is a process that takes time and dedication to build on who you are inside the shell and allow it to influence who you present yourself as in the world. Graciousness is an evolutionary process moving from compassion to graciousness. Compassion, on the other hand, has become the word of choice in our society. Compassion requires judgment: feeling for the other person, walking in the other person's shoes, or leaning into understanding what another person is going through to decide how you will offer support, love, or understanding. Compassion requires that a person act, whether in feelings, words, actions, or monetarily, based on what they are judging or told to judge, what they may pity, or what they feel is needed for another person. In this instance, compassion disempowers the individual you so desire to help. Since compassion doesn't necessarily work in the way we intend it to, compassion may cause depression and bring harm to you and to others.

Graciousness, on the other hand, empowers you and others. Graciousness is deeper and more meaningful than compassion. In today's society, a sweet, loving, kind, and giving person who dedicates themselves to helping others may be seen as compassionate. However, this person, in fact, may be driven by graciousness.

By being gracious, you offer acceptance to the intended individual without judgment or pity.

In graciousness, you can have a deep sense of awareness, support others the way they choose and gain an understanding of whether you can be of assistance. There may be others who are better suited to handle this situation graciously. Being in Graciousness allows us to protect what is within our shell and accept what is within another's. It requires that you are sovereign, meaning you have complete and utter authority and independence over you. Sovereignty doesn't mean you are selfish or self-involved. Being gracious means you have a deep connection with the truth of who you are: your soul's essence, knowing, unique pulse. It also means that you protect the truth of who you are by being sovereign requiring that you take full responsibility for yourself. You are responsible for the way you present yourself outside your Gracious Shell, which includes your body, your mind, and the energy you send out to the world—your thoughts, emotions, beliefs, vibes, and responses.

Let's break this down further. Compassion literally means "to suffer together." Among researchers who study emotion, compassion is defined as the feeling that arises when you are confronted with another's suffering and feel motivated to relieve that suffering. According to apa.org,[3] "compassion is a strong feeling of sympathy with another person's feelings of sorrow or distress, usually involving a desire to help or comfort that person." Based on the theory of compassion, unless you feel another's suffering, you may not be motivated to help that person. What, then, would happen to those less fortunate than you if you did not feel compassion? How do you really know they are less fortunate? And will you allow the intended to speak and tell you what they need instead of what you want? Consider that what you want for another person does not align with what they want for themselves.

Society pushes compassion, and unfortunately, compassion, in its purest definition, does not support our ability to remain sovereign, to remain in our truth. Compassion can contain elements of graciousness,

45

such as empathy and kindness. However, it is the other qualities, such as judgment, righteousness, and pity, that harm others.

Evolving into graciousness allows you to easily move in and out of any situation with kindness, serenity, and purity that brings no harm to you and leaves no harm to others.

Graciousness is an evolutionary concept that supports our sovereignty and presents a beautiful opportunity to release compassion's tight boundaries over us and others. You don't need compassion to be a good person; you need graciousness. We invite you to consider replacing compassion with a stronger, more empowering concept that guides you in all you do for yourself and for others—Graciousness. By becoming stronger in graciousness, meaning raising your Gracious Quotient, you become more empowered to be equally gracious to yourself as you are to others. The impact is that we can bring forth all our blessings in a more pure, supportive, and helpful way. First, consider the difference between the well-beaten path of compassion and the new paradigm of graciousness. It is a mind shift that will broaden your life—each moment, each day, and each year.

Practice: Exploring Compassion

◊ To understand when compassion is not helpful, start

with when you thought compassion was helpful. Grab and pen and paper or your computer and write about an experience where you thought being "compassion-ate" would be helpful but caused more harm uninten-tionally. Have you tried to comfort a person who has lost a loved one, and the person responded negative-ly? Your intended compassion (suffering together) was from your past experiences. You share your thoughts, stories of loss, and best wishes with that person. Instead of being comforted, this person responds negatively, turns pale, and looks devastated. You walk away feeling shocked and wonder why. Was the need to address the situation about you or about them? What was the story that developed in your head? How did you see them as part of your experience instead of respecting their experience?

◊ Have you ever offered an employee, a student, or another individual special treatment because they are not as "smart" or as physically able as others? You may have felt bad for them and had compassion for them because they were struggling to keep up, so you made excuses for them, spent valuable resources on them, or did some of the work for them. What judgment did you make in that situation? What story did you tell yourself about this other person? What pain did you feel, and how did your compassion show up? Is your compassion, then, actually harming that individual and the team? What was the prevalent emotion that led you to act on your compassion? Was it pity? Were you attempting to resolve the feelings of your own emotional discomfort?

Today, we have adopted the concept of compassion as a measure of our value. It is a common word choice in many spiritual traditions and is used as a point of reference for whether you align with those core values. Marketers have tapped into our emotional need to be seen as "good" and "giving." Marketers use compassion-driven campaigns yet, is it really making a difference? Or is it for your own gratification and validation? Have you considered that compassion is harming our society and potentially creating shame, humiliation, and entitlement in the same communities we are intending to help? Do you think you may know what is better for others? Are you aware that in doing so, you are defining what is "better" through the filter of your own view, your own judgments, your own pity, and your own biases? How can we help and offer support to those in need?

Graciousness allows us to enter a world where we all have sovereignty, acceptance, dignity, and caring. It allows us to see that we are all connected in some way. You may have already started along this evolutionary path without even realizing it. The following story may help clarify this concept.

Breanna noticed the homeless population near her home was settling into an encampment. Her heart ached, and she felt deeply sad about how they lived and wished they could have a proper home. Breanna had worked hard to own her home by working two jobs and being very careful with money. She occasionally stopped by and provided food for the homeless, but the more she did, the more depressed she became. She started to avoid the area, and anger started to settle in as she focused on how hard she worked and how long they stayed homeless. The depression was getting worse, and it was hard for her to sleep knowing the homeless were there and she couldn't do anything about it. She felt helpless and torn, guilty for what she had and what they didn't have.

Upon learning what graciousness was and how to live a gracious life, Breanna started moving toward a deeper understanding of graciousness, she started to feel lighter, sleep better, and could engage more with the homeless in a new way. She started to have greater respect for herself and her sovereignty, as well as those she met staying in the encampment. The individuals she met shared some thoughts and experiences with her, and what she discovered was that they had no desire to live like her or replicate that type of living. They wanted company and a warm meal but not her life. Breanna's judgment and pity harmed her mentally and physically, cheating her out of being gracious and free.

Explore Graciousness

When a compassionate situation you dealt with had a positive result, it is likely that you accepted the other person and offered what they actually stated they needed. Perhaps, you were being gracious at that moment and not "compassionate." Graciousness can offer a more solid, expansive way of being. Over our lifetime, we have been introduced to compassion as something to strive for—we are taught about it in our religions, schools, and relationships. And yet, compassion requires you to judge another's situation and act on it in a way that *you* believe is best, not what truly may be best.

Another way to define compassion is as sympathetic pity and concern for the sufferings or misfortunes of others. Would you appreciate others pitying you, telling you that you are not at their standard, therefore, you must accept help in the way they offer it?

Sometimes, what you may think is compassion, is really graciousness. Grab pen and paper or your computer and write about an experience where you thought you were being compassionate and it worked out well.

◊ Define the situation. Clearly identify what made you compassionate and who you were focused on with your compassion.

◊ How did you recognize the feeling of compassion? Was it driven by you or by a story you were told?

◊ How, then, did you respond to the situation?

◊ Did you make an impact? What was the impact on you? What was the impact on the person you were being compassionate with?

◊ Can you identify which components of your "compassion" were part of graciousness and which were compassionate?

Graciousness is defined as being kind and accepting, while compassion takes away dignity and respect for two simple reasons—judgment and pity.

Compassion	Graciousness
Literally means to suffer together.	Kindness and generosity of spirit.
You are confronted with another's suffering and feel motivated to relieve that suffering.	Does not require judgment to become motivated to offer support, love, or understanding.
Sympathetic pity and concern for the sufferings or misfortunes of another.	No longer relevant that you understand another, know what it feels like to be in their shoes, or that you must stretch your imagination to secure an understanding of what another needs.
You act, whether in words, action, or monetarily, based on your perception.	It requires you to ACCEPT other people for who they are.
Requires that you judge another based on what you see and that you have sympathetic pity for another.	There is no illusion of judgment, and there is acceptance for a person just as they are. You are not defining them through a filtered lens of your beliefs, ideals, and values. *Exception
Disempowers people.	Empowers people.

Compassion is ultimately a difficult way to be for everyone involved. *However, there are clearly situations where you must respond quickly to another without their permission or approval and while using your best judgment. Those situations include those who cannot think for themselves and/or depend on you for their well-being due to, for example, a critical health issue, mental illness, or life-threatening situation. This would also include young children and those who cannot speak for themselves. There are also situations where you can accept who another person is, however, you may not find them or their behavior acceptable and, therefore, will be unable to honor that person. For example, an individual may have intentions to hurt us, themselves or others.

Jonathan is an addict and has caused his family financial and emotional harm. His family doesn't give up on him and has offered support in paying for rehab, shelter, and food. Jonathan has lost control of his life and refuses to participate in his recovery. With graciousness, the family can accept this addiction and no longer honor Jonathan's choices. Therefore, the family faces a moment of choice. Are they the right team to help him, or are there others more capable who can intervene and make a difference?

Graciousness requires that you stay in sovereignty and are intentionally attuned to what supports your ability to be gracious. To stay in graciousness, you must protect all that is within the shell and maintain its sovereignty. This will enable you to have deep knowledge of yourself, thereby quickly self-correcting in new situations where you could potentially misstep and lose sovereignty. You will still feel a push and pull to do what others want you to do—but you will be able to resist the urge to hand over to another what is rightfully yours and what is rightfully your responsibility. You will have the strength to uncover what is best for you in the purest way.

Beyond Mindfulness

It is sometimes difficult to find the time to get to know your soul and be sovereign. A key to exploring your soul is to witness what you engage with, what is happening around you, how you respond, and what emotions are telling you. Your soul is your foundation. A concept that has been integrated into our lives is mindfulness; it is talked about in every facet of life—school, in therapy, at work, etc. Mindfulness is not graciousness, however, it can be helpful in being gracious. Mindfulness, according to the Mayo Clinic, is a type of meditation in which you focus on being intensely aware of what you're sensing and feeling in the moment without interpretation or judgment. Practicing mindfulness involves breathing methods, guided imagery, and other practices to relax the body and mind and help reduce stress.[4] Mindful.org explains that mindfulness is the basic human ability to be fully present, aware of where we are and what we're doing, and not overly reactive or overwhelmed by what's going on around us.[5]

Somatic mindfulness is another popular modality to help a person learn to step back from what their mind is telling them and instead observe the feeling or experience, feel it, and release it. Once it is released, the person consciously decides what they want to do instead of automatically falling into long-standing patterns.[6]

Mindfulness is one possible step toward graciousness from the perspective that we must take our time to know who we are, what impacts us, and how we would like to respond.

Graciousness, however, goes beyond the mind and body and into the inner part of the shell. The evolution from compassion to mindfulness and into graciousness will allow you to walk through life with a deep love and acceptance for yourself and, at the same time, a deep love and acceptance for all individuals.

What if our culture integrated this concept and gave a voice to who we really are as individuals, not how well we conform to traditional ways of being with rules that can potentially harm our society, our families, and ourselves? We have become attuned to what the culture[7] tells us, what our parents have shared, and even the career we trained for. As we expand our graciousness, we acknowledge what we are truly attuned to.

Attunement is when an individual knowingly or unknowingly accepts the rules, beliefs, values and essence of a culture, family, or person.

Culture has been called "the way of life for an entire society" and is passed down from generation to generation. As such, it includes codes of manners, dress, language, religion, rituals, art, norms of behavior, such as law and morality, and systems of belief.

Attunement has happened for us based on our family's way of being, culture, and religion. Based on these sources of foundational attunement, we know we belong because we follow the rules. So, why then, are many of us lonely when we follow the path we were attuned to as children or as adults? Perhaps, elements of this attunement go against who we truly are. Attunement, as the basis for sovereignty, means we decide what we will continue to be attuned to, what we will adjust, and what we will no longer support. This will release the longing—a depression of sorts—the yearning for something yet undiscovered. Given that many of us have not been attuning consciously, it may feel like we have no choice but to spend a lifetime trying to understand what is missing. As we grow and seek a meaningful life, we generally strive to unearth the hidden knowledge of who we truly are and what our purpose is.

We experience our human existence based on that to which we have attuned. As we release attunements that are no longer important, we slip out of old stale boundaries into a new, freer, and more expansive way of living. In our lives, there may be an intense fear of the consequences if we don't follow the rules; therefore, we find ways to manage the environment to get what we want, to feel safe and in control, and feed our ego so it doesn't face the loneliness and pain. Authentic attunement brings you to sovereignty, where you can reach higher levels of graciousness and, as a result, can see expansive opportunities where your blessings will make an impact, where you can create your future from a place of security, tenderness, and knowing. You, then, have the opportunity to reach the true meaning of your life.

Becoming More Sovereign

Sovereignty is a self-governing state. You, as your true authentic self, have complete and utter authority and independence over your thoughts, feelings, actions, mistakes, successes, and creations. You truly know who you are, what you are attuned to, and you gain higher levels of graciousness. You have a new understanding of your response, which has nothing to do with others and has everything to do with you. This doesn't mean you are selfish or self-involved. It means that what lies within the Gracious Shell is now influencing you and connecting you to what lies outside of the shell. Every person has the right to sovereignty and without accepting your sovereignty you will give up what you are truly here to be. By being sovereign, you will have the strength to uncover what is best for you in an authentic way. It is about finding kindness, firmness, and generosity in the space around you so that your blessings can manifest as needed. Sovereignty isn't for the mind; it is for your soul. Sovereignty allows information to be transferred from within your soul to your outer authentic self. There are no consequences for being sovereign. In fact, just the opposite is true–it opens up your entire life and rewards you in endless ways.

Practice: Attunement

The following practice can help you identify the source of your attunements, where they come from, and whether they are helpful. So grab a notepad and pen and consider the following.

If attunement was like clothing, how many layers are you wearing before you get to the real you? Do you have some layers that are thick wool coats? Summer linen shirts? Imagine a shirt as the religion in which you were raised in. Imagine a jacket as your parents' rules, or a hat as your career, and how you need to behave as you head out into the workforce. Imagine several scratchy shirts as a community where people are not supportive. Imagine a soft shirt as your favorite aunt who smiles at you with tenderness and joy as you share a story. When you think about attunements, consider your memories, what you want to cherish, and the values and belief systems you want to bring forward. Think about each clothing item as an attunement representing different aspects of your life. Heavy, uncomfortable, tight shirts that no longer support you represent what you need to start letting go. Do these conflict with your true self? Those shirts that are soft and fitting are what you may want to hold on to and may represent your true self.

1. Think about all the rules you live by—do this over a week.

2. Looking at those rules, ask yourself where did they come from?

3. Make a table with seven columns (see illustration below), and in the first column, list the rules you can identify today. In the second column, list where this attunement came from. In the third column, list whether you have agreed to this attunement.

4. Add the following three columns with the heading of "Keep", "Revise", and "Release".

5. Add a seventh column called "Sovereign". This column is designated for yes or no so that you can begin to understand where sovereignty exists for you.

6. Ask yourself the following questions. Do you believe these rules? Do they feel authentic to you today?

7. As you get to know your true self, regularly return to your chart and identify where you might want to keep, change, or release your attunement.

Rules you live by currently	Where did attunement come from?	Have you agreed to this attunement?	Keep	Revise	Release	Sovereign
Children are very precious.	Grew up this way—my family of origin enjoyed children.	I didn't think about it as it was natural—but yes, I agree.	Yes	No	No	Yes
The environment needs to be protected.	Grew up appreciating nature and the earth and feeling connected to it.	Yes. It feels very natural to me.	Yes	No	No	Yes

As you reflect, please notice that you can make changes or keep what you would like within your daily life, and decide where you can enhance your day or free yourself from attunements that no longer serve you.

In Summary

The evolution of compassion to graciousness requires that you understand what you are attuned to so that you can reach the sovereignty, which is required for higher levels of graciousness. There is no absolute right way of being, you decide what is in your soul. Start first, with recognizing past attunements, decide what may or may not work for you today, and then bring out your soul's essence, knowing and pulse. Over time and with practice, you will reach sovereignty with ease, where you authentically live your soul's purpose.

CHAPTER FOUR
The Gracious Quotient

The Gracious Quotient is designed to help us think more about how gracious we are in any given moment. It allows us to understand where we fall within a range of graciousness. Being in the higher levels of graciousness means being free to offer your blessings to yourself and others, to connect, have more fulfilling experiences, and trust, knowing that you see yourself and others in the purest way possible. At higher levels, your soul becomes most present.

The Gracious Quotient is an approach to stretch your consciousness, broaden your abilities, and offer you the greatest gift of creating the life you want. Becoming gracious allows all the energy around you to become settled, peaceful, authentic, and in a state of Divine acceptance. Graciousness means that you accept yourself and others in the present moment. The Gracious Quotient offers you information and insight about where you are and allows you to consciously choose what level you would like to be in. Most of us ebb and flow from lower to higher levels of the Gracious Quotient, with level 10 being the highest level of graciousness and level 1 being the very lowest.

Graciousness is a capability of your soul, not a capability of your mind or intellect. While mental capability is necessary for increasing your level of graciousness so that you can discern where you are and how to use the approach, the more critical element is that your soul is fully present and working toward its full blessings. When you are operating in full graciousness, you naturally become highly gracious. Simply stated, graciousness comes from the ability to be in your highest blessings—to feel satisfied without others validating or appreciating you.

Graciousness requires that you are as equally gracious to yourself as you are to others.

If you don't use your blessings, then graciousness quickly falls away. When you lack trust, you are not giving yourself, or others, a chance to succeed. When you are in the lower levels of graciousness, you begin entering a darker world where you cannot offer your blessings to yourself or others. By expanding into higher levels of graciousness, you can easily offer blessings.

The 10 Levels

There are 10 levels of the Gracious Quotient. Graciousness is impacted by what you believe, how you embrace emotions and values, how pure you are in your actions, whether you send out positive or negative currents, whether you are sovereign and, whether you are in your essence and conscious of your energy.

*The greater our graciousness, the greater the oppor-
tunity to find the freedom to offer our blessings.*

As you read through the levels, remember to fully
embrace yourself exactly where you are. No one is
expected to be in the higher levels from the start, nor
should you expect that of yourself. Wherever you are
now is your starting point. You will gain traction as you
shed those habits, beliefs, and behaviors that limit
your Gracious Quotient and become more attuned to
what works for you—you will then be free to create the
life you want.

Each of the 10 levels has its own unique characteris-
tics. You can find yourself at any level throughout the
day as you face new situations. You may remain at
one level more frequently than others. It is essential
to challenge yourself to be fully authentic and honest
about your level of graciousness at any moment. This
way, you can have full authority over your time in the
lower levels and how you move to higher levels. At any
moment, you can move from level 8 to level 4. Or, you
may find yourself in level 3 and know you must move
into level 5. As you practice, you will start to self-identify where you fall at any given moment, and you will
gain the skills to move up the levels as you practice
using the approach. It is the skills you gain by applying

what you learn that frees you from self-judgment and self-criticism.

Graciousness Level 10

The highest level of graciousness is when you have the most profound connection to your soul. At this level, your actions are in one hundred percent alignment with your soul, and there is no conflict within. There is no judgment or preconceived notions. You see others and yourself as you truly are. You are experiencing full authority of yourself, full sovereignty, and the deepest level of purity. You completely trust your own knowing with the answers needed for your life. Your goal is to unite with integrity, dignity, and respect with sincere humility.

Individuals at level 10 have the deepest level of spiritual connection and the ability to remove themselves from the demands of being human (i.e., Buddha or Jesus or other Divine source). Being at level 10 means existing fully in the Divine's purpose, where all becomes one and is seen as interconnected. Your thought pattern is one of achieving the highest level of acceptance, where you accept all individuals and do not judge. While you know "right" from "wrong" (discernment), you trust that other individuals are or have the potential to also be at a level 10.

You are not concerned with judgment, preconceived

notions of grandeur, or being different and better than others. You don't feel compelled to influence others, take ownership, or think you are independent of others. You are not self-involved, righteous, or rigid and have no attachment to the outcome of a plan or action. Level 10 is not fear-driven in any way, nor nebulous, difficult, or emotional. It may appear that at level 10 you are detached from the rules of society and the attunement of your culture and world. However, this is not the case. Level 10 simply knows the deep interconnectivity of all souls and dismisses the need to be part of the permanence that so many individuals seek.

Achieving this level is rare, and while it is a highly worthy goal, it is challenging to sustain as it is hard to live only in a soulful manner. Our human body and those around us require us to live in the human world to survive. Level 10 expresses that we are in resounding unison with the Divine, that everyone is seen as a soul and honored as a soul. Every individual is accepted just as they are with all humility possible.

Graciousness Level 9

At level 9, you are deeply connected to the Divine and see others as the authentic self that they are. While level 9 is also difficult to maintain for very long, it is easier to achieve than level 10. You have a deep sense of knowing and confidence that this knowing is pure and Divine. While you may be curious, have some

G

preconceived notions, and are influenced by the world around you, you accept and respect others as they are.

When hurt by others, you may have fleeting moments of despair and pain, but your acceptance of individuals is relatively high. You trust your knowing. You quickly pick up on what an individual is saying as you hear them in a way where all their emotion is stripped away from their words and energy—you hear the words but not the inflections. You appreciate what others are saying without the influence they are trying to convey. You see through the veil of others' emotions and into the purity of their expression—whether positive or negative—for what it is. In your humility, you can quickly restate another's words exactly how they meant it.

Moving from level 9 to 10 is hard and fleeting. While we have a strong level of respect for ourselves and others, a strong connection to the Divine, live in integrity and knowing, and have a high need to unite, we still need to influence others. We have the fundamental belief that we must be gracious to others and equally gracious to ourselves. We tend to use more of our authentic selves when speaking or influencing others.

To move up a level, we must avoid influencing others. At level 9, we are not heavily concerned with emotions, hurdles, being nebulous, righteous, or self-involvement, and we tend to stay away from rigid and organized thought groups as we don't need strong association with others. At level 9, we would rather spend time bringing others together and uplifting the energy of others and the group. However, there is no desire to be in the group. Moving down levels is relatively easy as we judge, have self-doubt, fear, and ways that are the attunement of the past start to seep back in.

Graciousness Level 8

Level 8 is marked by a high hunger for knowledge and curiosity about self, others, and the Divine. You have an almost insatiable appetite for seeking - you seek to understand. At level 8, your curiosity is at an all-time high, and you want to know why people do what they do. "Why is this individual doing this?" "Why is this individual feeling that?"

While you are high in acceptance of others, purity, wanting to unite, and humility, you find yourself allowing preconceived notions to find their way in. You acknowledge that you can be somewhat judgmental and work hard to keep it in check. You can look at someone's expression and determine whether their actions or words are pure. You want to influence others to become more like you regarding acceptance, curiosity about the "why," and the desire to be connected to the Divine. You want to understand how another thinks and feels, how they present themselves and their responses, and you want to judge. Yet, you do this with a pure heart and open mind. You do this because you want your discoveries to bring enlightenment and more information.

At level 8, it is imperative to comprehend our hunger to understand, to see more, to be more, and to find vitality in our knowledge. The way to increase our gracious level is to understand that while we may struggle with our knowing and integrity, we have a strong balance and a deep desire for dignity, trust, connection, and seeing people as their authentic selves. We understand we must let go of the need for things to stay the same and the profound struggle we may have with loss. Moving up to level 9 will require that we accept others as they are, practice ways to respond respectfully and humbly, release what we have been attuned to through our lives that no longer support graciousness and focus on a deep connection with the Divine through the practice you determine is right for you.

Graciousness Level 7

Level 7 is characterized as being curious with a deep hunger for knowledge. You strive for humility and deep acceptance of yourself and others while desiring strong influence over outcomes. You notice and experience a significant drop from level 8 concerning sovereignty, purity, trust, the desire to unite, integrity, and knowing. That said, you profoundly understand that you have an authentic self and want to share your thoughts about it and have a relationship with the Divine.

You are heavily influenced by others you want to be like and can be somewhat stubborn on this stance. You have strong preconceived notions, the desire to be right, and the desire to be very influential. With this high need for influence, you are also focused on the outcome of your influence on others and strive to take ownership of the outcome. You have an increased curiosity and hunger for information and will dive deep to gain information from those you think are acting in a way inconsistent with what you want or expect to see.

Whether in your mind or through talking with others, you constantly seek the answers to "Who are you?" "What are you?" "Why are you acting like this?" You may likely lose a little respect for those you see as influential since they may not have the "right" answers. You also can quickly lose dignity in the way you approach yourself, others, and issues. You do have a desire for connection to the Divine and to humility; however, you may find that you do not achieve what you wanted as your days are filled with your interest in others. At this level, you are not always conscious of your responses to situations, yet you always strive to be accepting while fighting the judgment that seems to find its way in.

At level 7, we can move up or down a level quite easily. We feel well on the path of connection to our authentic selves and have a sense of balance and graciousness in what we do and how we treat ourselves and others. Elevating to the next level is not difficult if we stay open to being sovereign so that our true authentic selves can become a more significant part of ourselves. That said, slipping down a level or two is also relatively easy since we still have remnants of being more self-involved than self-aware, righteous and rigid in our views, and emotional and fear-driven relating to change. To move up a level, we can use the practices in Chapter 9 to help us become more accepting, gain humility, and free ourself of our curiosity and the need to be influential. This will also prevent us from slipping down to the lower levels of graciousness.

Graciousness Level 6

Level 6 is typically marked by being belief-oriented and firmly attached to living and responding in a very static and specific way. At level 6, you are, for the most part, a happy-go-lucky person going with the flow, following the rules of your family, community, and any organizations you belong to. You have some insight into your authentic self and appreciate the need to be more authentic. Because you like rules, you tend to be influenced by others who appear to have the answers.

You have a strong focus on preconceived notions, a desire to be influential, are more self-involved than self-aware, and have a tendency toward righteousness in your views. You need to keep things the same, as change is difficult for you.

At this level, you attach to the outcome you want to see within yourself and with others. You strive to be humble and in unison with your Divine purpose. However, you keep sabotaging opportunities for enlightenment. There is intense confusion on how to soothe or smooth situations you find yourself in. Your sovereignty is tested, and you see others as people rather than souls. At level 6, your humility can dip, and you are torn between whether it is better to unite or divide based on self-righteous principles.

Level 6 is typically when we are firm in our beliefs and attached to a specific way of doing things, so we find it challenging to maintain a strong balance. We understand that the relationship we have with the Divine is purely between the Divine and us.

We can easily move from this level to a higher level by remembering that our sacred relationship does not need to be validated by others. Through practice, we can identify that we are at this level and can move up a level by simply placing ourselves within the Gracious Shell and remembering the only source of truth is not outside of us, not in our minds or bodies, but within our soul.

Graciousness Level 5

Level 5 is marked by looking at the world and working to figure out what piece belongs to you. Most individuals are at this level at least a few times a day. At level 5, you are more concerned with your day-to-day life and trying to identify what is yours and your allotted tasks as part of the system (work, school, home, etc.). To identify what is yours, you have a sense of self, a sense of risk and reward, and a sense of financial well-being. You are more focused on ownership of things and people. You have preconceived fixed notions, feel independence is critical, and fear you will lose what is yours.

You tend to be heavily focused on keeping your life the same, in the way you want it to be. Fear of change is a common theme for you. Fear and consequence drive how you make decisions—"If I do this, what will I lose?" or "What are the consequences?" At this stage, your focus is on scarcity, not having enough, so you tend to focus on dividing others and communities so that you have your "fair" share. You are influenced by what others think and say, and while you understand that you have a true authentic self, it is hard to fit in the time to figure it all out.

Your relationship with the Divine is through religion or other structured means, and there are rules to follow. You feel you are part of society more than you are part of your own soul and can become heavily involved with what is happening and how you behave within your society. While you seek respect and dignity and want to accept others, you struggle with staying sovereign. Consequently, you experience lower levels of purity, trust, and power. To you, power is only held by the authorities and is not an option for you to hold yourself.

We know when we are in level 5 and can, if self-aware, easily slip to level 6 by managing our thoughts and shining a light on what scarcity means. We can be pretty nimble in this phase and easily rectify the issues by reflecting on how blessed we are. We know and can trust there will be enough for all of us. While it is equally easy to slip back into level 4 without self-awareness, we can quickly move up a level from a level 5 with focus on purity and trust within ourselves.

Graciousness Level 4

Level 4 is characterized by judgment, demand for immediate gratification, and a territorial nature. Level 4 is something we have all experienced intensely—where we are extraordinarily judgmental. You may talk about what another person did or judge what your neighbors are doing and hold it against them. At level

G

4, you tend to judge people to see whether they fit into your definition of "right." You cannot tap into your authentic self easily, and it is hard to comprehend this idea. You may tend to say things like, "I don't like this person because..." "I cannot seem to talk with the Divine—I don't have a connection at all," or "I wish things were like they used to be when I was young— when I was cared for and sheltered."

Your thoughts lose purity and trust, and you become focused on what, when, and how you want specific outcomes. It is a level of demanding immediate justice, gratification, and answers. You find you have become rigid, with tight reins on ownership (this is mine, not yours), and if another person doesn't fit your description of what you have decided as acceptable, you reject them. This level is challenging for you and for those around you. You may not clearly see that you have hurt others by your lack of acceptance and respect and wonder what you did to deserve their wrath. You begin to move into an emotional state that can start to resemble a tornado and may find yourself being nebulous and unclear on what you really think.

This level can create more damage because others may see you as somewhat good and want to believe in you. However, you may twist and manipulate their energy to get what you want, with little care for what others get. At this level, you have little desire for purity, integrity, uniting, humility, and trust and are seen as self-involved, rigid, and righteous—you want everything to stay the same—"your same".

Everyone experiences level 4 intensely at one time or another, but being so rigid and controlling in our thoughts and actions long-term can damage us and our relationships, so the goal is to move quickly up the scale to at least level 5, preferably 6. We have the skills and wherewithal to move up a level by being self-aware and recognizing that this territorial nature is part of our human side but that there is much more to us than thoughts and emotions.

Graciousness Level 3

Level 3 is characterized as a feeling of powerlessness and fear as you see only what others have shown you. Level 3 is filled with entrapment and doesn't allow you to reach very high. While you may desire to free yourself, you are trapped in your attunement to your upbringing, carrying values and beliefs that prevent you from being sovereign. You are completely unaware that you don't see clearly at all. Sovereignty eludes you, so you find yourself powerless and beholden to fear. You cannot hold onto the idea of your true authentic self or even the ideal of your true authentic self. Instead, you only see what others have told you to see.

You may not be aware of your intense feelings of insecurity, but you do find yourself caring more for your own security than for your loved one's security. You do whatever it takes to find security, including intentionally manipulating others to get what you want. This level is tricky because you become so emotionally charged that no one can say anything right to help you, nor can you talk yourself out of this level. Everywhere you look, life feels like a challenge. You may be severely depressed and even move into self-harm as you wonder why you are precluded from being part of life and events. You want everything to stay the same and want others to stand still as not to disrupt your day. You hold others responsible for what you do not have, and you blame others for a perceived disruption of your static world.

This is a tough level because you sense something isn't quite right but cannot see that it comes from you, from not being able to acknowledge that your authentic self exists. You desire to accept what is and want to be respected because you believe you have dignity in your position. However, the desire is quickly overrun by the injustice of what should be going on around you, creating the perception of an unsafe situation for you. Your curiosity, emotional intelligence, and desire to be influential are missing. You become deeply attached to a position of extreme independence, ownership, and righteousness—you will not listen to anyone and have a rigid sense of how things should be done including the outcome. Anything that starts to change can cause extreme stress, and fear-driven emotions control your day.

We all know people like this, and in fact, we may find ourselves at this level quite frequently. It is in our best interest to move quickly out of this level. If we stay in this level too long, we will need help to guide us into higher levels of graciousness. When we are in a higher level of graciousness with more self-awareness, we may choose to prepare for this lower level so that we can move out of it quickly. Even though we may need help, we may not be open to it at this level, so we must decide what will help us. We may decide that our self-talk is unhelpful, so creating a few mantras or sayings such as "I am free to be me" or "I am valuable because I have a soul" may be the best solution for moving up a level.

Graciousness Level 2

In level 2, emotional needs overwhelm you at the expense of your authentic self and can create confusion, lack of focus, and awareness of others. You will find you feel constantly stuck and sidetracked. You cannot seem to focus. You may feel torn most of the time, trying to figure out what to do next. It is hard to acknowledge that you have an authentic self. You find it difficult to seek help, or even believe others help.

G

You experience deep, intense emotions that dictate your actions. In other words, the density of emotions forms a cloud around you, so it is hard to see anything other than these emotions. You focus on one way of doing things, your way, as you have become so rigid in your thoughts and actions that you cannot see a healthier way. You are harshly judgmental with a need to make fun of, bully, and take what you believe is rightfully yours. You see others as enemies who want to cause you pain. You believe that others want to take what is "yours." You may even fear for your safety most of the time. You feel you cannot be there for another person unless there is something concrete in it for you, such as a financial payment or gift. Seeing anything soul-based is challenging.

Sovereignty, purity, and humility are traits you may want to consider or something you want to attain. However, the nebulous nature of where you are at this level makes it difficult to move past your focus on what you see as the "right way."

Level 2, also happens to us all, perhaps, though not as frequently. It is a challenging level and virtually impossible to move out of if we stay at this level too long because we get trapped in highly dense emotions that are not easy to navigate. It is easy to slip into level 1 from here if we cannot see what our emotions are trying to tell us. At this level, a person is in a nebulous state where clarity is not readily achievable. Others find us difficult to be around as they don't know what to say to soothe or help us. We can move up a level without help if we find a way to reach out to and appreciate support from others. When we are in a higher level of graciousness with more self-awareness, we may choose to prepare for this lower level in order to move out of it quickly. An option is to leave visual reminders of our authentic selves, such as notes, affirmations, and images, or ask a loved one to remind us that we are loved to help us move out of this temporary level, i.e. white ribbons remind us of purity.

Graciousness Level 1

Level 1 is characterized by satisfying your desires at the expense of others and harboring ill will or holding grudges against those who resist you. Even if you haven't witnessed this person, you have undoubtedly heard of them. Level 1 is the darkest of levels and is characterized by the desire to harm others either for the sake of harm or to satisfy your own needs. You do not have the slightest desire to be your authentic self, making this the most challenging level to move out of.

In level 1, you have lost humility and the ability to care for others, sometimes even to care for yourself. You will not be aware that you are in level 1 and are so troubled with how things "should" be that there is no thought of moving out of this level. At this level, you will satisfy your desires—whatever those might be. You are frozen to the outside world and yourself. You feel powerful in your own stance and may even be proud of your manipulations and cunning ways to get what you want. Sovereignty, purity, and humility are not traits of this level since, in these moments, you are self-righteous, and focused only on your own needs.

A person at level 1 is often predatory and shows no remorse or care for any harm caused to others, just a need to satisfy their desires at any cost. It is extremely challenging to move from level 1 alone and to do so requires interventions, intense love from others, and a willingness for others to sacrifice sometimes, at a high cost, to help you move from this level. More importantly, for those interventions to work, also requires the ability for self-awareness, which at this level may be lacking or completely hidden in the dark energies that have pervaded your being. Divine intervention is always required to move a person out of level 1.

In Summary

These levels are a guide meant to help you find a path toward higher levels of graciousness and thus regain back is rightfully yours, the ability to be fully integrated with your soul. You will have the freedom to engage with your soul, your true authentic self. We all move through various levels daily, even from moment to moment. We may recognize times of intense joy as

well as ill will. There are many ways to remain in higher levels of graciousness and you may increase your
gracious quotient with more awareness and
practice.

CHAPTER FIVE
How to Prepare for Graciousness

Considering a new concept to bring into your life takes time. Living a life of graciousness is a long-term endeavor, and it may take you years to integrate all the methods and move quickly up the scale. We are all human and have many trials and tribulations that will sometimes make our world look sideways. The passing of our loved ones and questioning why, the break-up of a long-term relationship, the pressures of raising a family, the stress of work, the political and social unrest, fears of violence in our communities, and the fear of health issues have many of us questioning what is really happening in our world, in our communities, and in our homes. This fear is making it hard to feel safe enough to seek freedom, and yet more and more individuals are taking the brave step in finding their path to freedom.

Our society places high value on attributes that contribute to personal success, such as IQ and EQ (emotional intelligence). Success is equated with financial achievement. At the same time, we are told we need to have compassion and sacrifice for the benefit of others and this can cause many of us to feel guilty and ashamed. What if we evolved to walk through life in a gracious way where we have a deep love and respect for ourselves and, simultaneously, are deeply loving and respectful of all souls? What if communities integrated graciousness and gave voice to who we really are, not how well we conform to old ways of being, old rules that hurt our society, families, and souls? We have become attuned to what the culture tells us, what our parents have shared, and even what career we trained for.

As a result, many of us feel lonely when we follow the path to which we were attuned to as children. Perhaps, because those concepts and ideals are not part of our soul's purpose. Not being attuned to our souls creates a longing, a depression of sorts, a yearning for something yet undiscovered. Childhood attunement brought to us some ways that work and others that likely won't work in the best interest of our soul any longer, so we start to search for meaning and purpose often directionless.

But what if you could tap into that feeling of loneliness and be propelled into a recognition of your soul, your purpose? Given that many of us have not been consciously attuned to our souls, what other choice do we have than to spend a lifetime trying to understand the soul? As we grow and seek meaningful adulthood, we generally strive to understand what it means to "open the door to our soul" and how to cultivate the deepest understanding of our soul's essence, knowing, and pulse in our lives.

What happens when we attune to our soul? Will we be able to visibly see the energy of each soul? What would you look like to others since emotions and outward appearance are no longer seen as who you really are? What would others look like to you? Knowing that we are part of the Divine, would our souls shine so bright that we would be blinding to others? How far would our lights shine? How would others see our beautiful energy? Today, we are recognizable to each other based on our physical features, our voices, and our choices. What if we could actually feel the energy and the light of our souls and of other souls? How would we then respond to others?

Guidance to Higher Levels

Think of the descriptions of the ten levels as a guide intended to help you find a path to higher levels of graciousness and thus regain what is rightfully yours, the ability to be fully integrated with your soul. You will be free to engage with your Gracious Shell. We all move through various levels of graciousness daily. In any given moment, we may recognize moments of intense joy as well as ill-will. There are many ways to remain in higher levels of graciousness, and you may increase your gracious quotient with more awareness and practice.

Graciousness is a concept that may take time to understand and get comfortable with, especially as you evolve from compassion to graciousness. Achieving a life of graciousness is a long-term endeavor that requires time, effort, and patience. It may take weeks, months, or even years to fully integrate the necessary tools to elevate yourself to higher levels of graciousness. As human beings, we all face challenges and obstacles that can make our world seem chaotic and uncertain. Whether it's the loss of a loved one, the end of a long-term relationship, the stress of raising a family, the demands of work, the political and social turmoil, or the fear of health issues, these trials can leave us feeling overwhelmed and uncertain about our future.

However, despite these challenges, more and more people are taking courageous steps towards achieving their desired level of freedom. It can be difficult to feel safe enough to pursue your goals when you're consumed by fear, but with persistence and determination, it's possible to overcome these obstacles and find your path to higher levels of graciousness.

Becoming gracious brings awareness to situations in life that cause us to become trapped in wanting to know why. The "why" question freezes us, causing discomfort, confusion, and frustration. Consider that you now have a moment of choice instead of a moment of confusion. The moment of choice allows you to move to higher levels of graciousness, and in a sense, you have graduated from and released what has trapped you. We each must find our own process. Graciousness will become naturally embedded in all you do. Remember, incorporating graciousness is on your terms and in your own time. In times of crisis, you may see an urgent need to do more work on graciousness, while in more settled times, you may naturally embrace graciousness and all its components. Some days you may accept spending a day at level 5 or even level 3. On other days, you may want to become free of the world's constraints, jump into the methods, and practice your skills to move up levels of graciousness.

Take time to embrace the methods and concepts of the Gracious Quotient so they work for you and your life.

Using the following practice can help you to increase your self-awareness and gain more perspective.

Practice: Shift your Focus

Being ready to adopt a more evolved way of living requires taking the time to be with a new awareness. As quickly as you can and without much thought, jot down the answers to each of the following questions. Don't look at your answers after you write them. Place them in a sealed envelope:

1. How much time can you dedicate to cultivating a new awareness each day?

2. On a scale of 1 to 10 (1 being minimal and 10 most significant), how pulled do you feel to move into a new awareness?

3. How often do you wish you would respond to situations differently?

4. Do you have relationships with people who will support your growth?

5. Can you be honest with yourself?

6. If no one else needs to see or understand you, what about you is critical to keep and/or change?

7. Are you willing to take the opportunity to experience what your emotions are telling you?

8. Do you believe you have the perseverance to elevate all areas of your life?

After a few weeks, answer the questions all over again. Open the first envelope and compare to your new responses. Do your answers match? What changes do you see? After answering the questions a second time, put those answers in an envelope and seal them again for another month. Keep repeating this practice until you feel you have made significant progress in your willingness and capability to embrace your new awareness.

Being Ready

Each of us moves up the Gracious Quotient in our own time. Your desire, willingness, and capability are essential to your success. While it would likely be a wonderful world if everyone adopted a gracious lifestyle, it is impossible to assume everyone will do so at the same time, if at all. Being in a place of readiness to adopt these concepts is imperative for your expansion. Research shows that when you are open to grasping and incorporating new skills, it will be much easier for you to adopt those skills.

Being ready means you:

◊ Have an awareness of your Gracious Shell, blessings, and soul.

◊ Have an undeniable pull to move forward.

◊ Realize that you want to be a person who wants to be "blessings-based," meaning you can freely share your blessings.

◊ Acknowledge and appreciate that you have

negatively affected others with some ungracious behaviors.

◊ Understand that there is tremendous support for living a life of blessings.

◊ Seek relationships that support and encourage you.

◊ Accept the need to substitute emotionally charged behaviors and thoughts for a blessings-based approach.

◊ Reduce your dependency on emotional behaviors and reinforce positive blessing-based approaches.

◊ Design your life so that you have reminders and cues to support and encourage graciousness.

In Summary

As we prepare to embrace graciousness, it is critical for you to keep reviewing and thinking about these ideas. Each person will have a different experience and that is exactly how it should be. No two people are alike, and no two souls are alike. It is best to do this work alone, taking time to move into your own level of Graciousness without judging or comparing where others are or how they should advance. The Gracious Quotient concept is filled with new ways of thinking, a language that you may not have been aware of, and practices that support you in awakening to this concept. When you feel overwhelmed and find the concepts confusing, we invite you to review the definitions in the addendum to help you gain clarity. In the next phase of the book, you will find the methods and guidance on how to integrate graciousness into everyday life. The methods to raise graciousness include:

◊ **The Current**—Acknowledging what type of current you are experiencing or stepping into and making a solid choice to maintain or improve.

◊ **Sovereignty**—Identify when you need to step back into sovereignty so that you can move up levels freely.

◊ **Belief Strands**—Decide what your belief strands are and identify which ones are activated in how you respond today and what belief strands will need to change to act in graciousness.

◊ **Emotions**—Use emotions as a teaching tool and not as an "I am" tool where others think you are your emotions.

◊ **Mantras**—Creating Mantras for manifesting what is in your best interest to keep you in a place of graciousness.

◊ **Moments of Choice**—Understanding that choices you make matter in how you stay at higher levels of graciousness.

PHASE II

Methods to Raise Graciousness

CHAPTER SIX
Raising your Gracious Quotient: Managing Current

The Gracious Quotient was designed to help you think more concisely about how gracious you are in any given moment and then adjust accordingly. It allows you to understand where you are within the range of graciousness. Being in the higher levels of graciousness means that you are free to connect, experience, and trust, knowing that you see your blessings in the purest way possible and that you see others in the purest way. In the higher levels of graciousness, you see the potential for all that you can be without judgement and without concern. You feel the fullness of your blessings and your capability to be who you really are. Living this way allows you to fully accept yourself and take personal responsibility while witnessing others doing the same.

Graciousness opens access to your full blessings and, thus, your essence, knowing and pulse. One key to raising your Gracious Quotient is aligning your soul with how you present yourself to others. This can only happen if what you show to others is attuned to your soul, which requires that you are both conscious of and able to manage the Current you emit. Your Current is heavily influenced by your intentions. Your intentions are dictated by your attunements, beliefs, and core values. The soul must have a more significant influence on our Current for us to stay sovereign, ultimately leading to our ability to be open enough to send our blessings to ourselves and those around us.

Current

Your Currents are fueled by your intentions and may not always be visible to you, but others may feel them and the Current of the room. A Current is commonly experienced as "reading the room" or "sensing what another feels." The Current is the vibe that pulsates around us. It is the energy of the room, of others, or the combination of others' energy that creates a Current. Most of us cannot deny "picking up on" what is happening energetically in a situation, as Currents have a life of their own and gain intensity depending on the intentions and can easily be misinterpreted. We witness Currents everywhere: in an emotional reaction; a facial expression; the anxiety of another; a person's tone of voice; a person's home; etc.

It is fruitless to think we can hide dense emotional thoughts as they show up in our Current.

Our voice is a critical element of the current, especially tone and pace. Our voice often changes as our intention changes, whether to influence, express love, express joy, or express despair. In the lower levels of the Gracious Quotient, we use our voice to influence or control individuals ninety percent of the time; that means we only have ten percent of the time to bring forth our truth and blessings. At lower levels, our voice can cause paranoia, tenseness, fear, frustration, and lack of awareness, in both us and others. Conversely, in the high levels of graciousness, our voices express an acceptance, is not trying to control or influence others, and send a Current of warmth, support, caring, and general overall grace.

Currents are deeply felt within the body, although it is trickier to accurately read other people's energy. In order to read a situation accurately, you must be aware of and manage your intentions, stories, and perceptions. The power of Currents can uplift, create peace and calm, or on the opposite end, create confusion and distortion for us within a matter of seconds. Without awareness, moods will shift and become captive to the Currents around us. It is in those moments that our levels of graciousness change without our awareness and our sovereignty slips. This means we must be hyper-aware and practice appreciating the Currents while not allowing those Currents to influence us. We all understand that we can influence others and bring excitement, life, passion, empowerment, and beyond all, blessings to others. Currents are external and do not emanate from the soul, although if we are conscious of our energy, we can and will affect change for the highest good of all of us.

We can intensify or turn down, the Currents of a room by changing our levels of graciousness. Be aware that Currents can become barriers and divert our focus away from the blessings we are here to bring.

A Current can be seen or felt in just about every-thing—the energy of music, water, anger, love, elec-tricity, plants, fire, wind, and the earth. This Current shows up in every second, every millisecond. Being aware, or conscious, of the Current within and around you will help you acknowledge how best to work with yours. You can choose to use your Current purposefully, to invoke graciousness, and to expand your blessings.

Practice: Becoming Aware of Currents

This practice will help you learn how to identify the Currents you sense in a room.

1. Gather a journal or piece of paper, something to write with, or your device.

2. Begin by making four sections on your paper (or screen) with the titles "Situation" "Alone," "With Others," and "Witness".

3. Find a place where you are not required to partic-ipate and where you can witness the Current of the room. This could be in your home, work, or a social setting. Ideally, you are first to the room, as this will

allow you to get the "lay of the land" and get a feel for the room's Current on its own. Place this information in the section "Situation".

4. As you sit alone, notice what is happening around you, in your mind and body, as you track your intentions and feelings with the room's Current. Then, under the section "Alone," write down your experience.

5. As others enter the room, start to notice what is happening for you and then slow this down by taking some deep breaths so that you can eliminate much of your own Current and then start to take notice of what others are bringing into the room. Write your observations under the section labeled "With Others."

6. Lastly, reflect on what happened during this exchange and write down what you witnessed in the "Witness" section. This is where you can learn more about what is happening with the Current and not each individual.

Typically, you change a Current by adding your emotions, intentions, and beliefs. Remember to separate what you believe about others based on their emotional responses, facial expressions, gestures, words, and intensity. Notice the current that is blending and swirling around the room. This way, you can focus purely on reading the Current and not the individuals. Here is an example of how this can work:

Situation:

Wake up and go to the kitchen to get coffee.

Alone:

I enter the room alone, and it feels peaceful. As I get my coffee, thoughts of the day start to enter, and I start to worry about the day—I recognize this and set my intention to slow down, breathe, and simply enjoy a fresh cup of coffee.

With Others:

My family enters the room, and the noise levels increase with movement and chatter. I become more alert, and my intention shifts to my family's needs. I start to scan the room for what is needed. I stop and let the room's Current be, meanwhile noticing what I am sensing.

Witness:

The Current is swirling with needs, a heightened sense of excitement, and the intention of setting expectations for the day. The Current is blending the output of others into one, and it looks like others are taking it in and responding nonverbally—shifting and moving seats, leaving the room, and looking around at the others. I notice I want to soothe, make ready, set the mood, or override the Current blending. As each person leaves, I notice the Current becomes less intense, and the Current comes back to a peaceful state. After some time, I reflect on the Current, the blending, and my response.

Another Example Is For A Work Situation

Situation:

Office meeting or at work.

Alone:

This doesn't allow for an option to be alone in the room.

With Others:

I am the fifth person entering the room. It feels suffocating and tense as I scan the room. I stop focusing on my own reaction and start focusing on the Current in the room.

Witness:

The Current gets thicker and more intense with more people entering the room. A shift happens when the boss enters. Part of the Current stills and part moves more slowly but with purpose. As the boss finishes and leaves the room, the Current relaxes, yet the voices of others start to increase in intensity and influence. The shift was from a sense of compliance to a sense of rebellion. Where did this come from?

Types of Currents

As you become more aware of the Current, you will be able to identify and acknowledge what type of Current you are experiencing and, if needed, decide to improve. The Current you or another person emits is an unseen energy you may or may not be conscious of. Currents can either support or interfere with your blessings. Currents can keep us stagnant or help us expand. Your thoughts, words, and actions are all a part of these Currents. If you are conscious about your Current, you can enter a room and either intensify or de-intensify the Current. It takes time to get in touch with the Current and identify where it falls daily or even momentarily.

The Current is transmitted through how we use emotions to elicit a desired reaction.

The Current is driven by the density or our intentions and emotions. You cannot hide the Current created by your intentions; you may be able to control how you deliver a message, but the Current carried with that message is clearly received by others. While imperfect, the following guide may be useful in recognizing where you are energetically and what you are signaling through the Currents. It is important to update or reframe your intentions as they ultimately change what you offer to your loved ones, community, and the world.

Density

Density refers to the intensity of emotions; we refer to high density as strong negative emotions such as worry and fear as well as strong positive emotions such as love and joy. When emotions are high, and thought patterns are deep, the density is high and negatively affects your soul's ability to express itself outwardly. This density dims the light of your soul and reduces our ability to be self-aware and sovereign, which then stunts our self-awareness, and we cannot fulfill our life's purpose. High density is like a million particles around you that you cannot see through, and you become fearful. Whereas, low density is a state were emotions and thoughts are lighter and less intense.

Getting Clear on Intentions

Your intention is your hope, aim, purpose, or desire. Intentions bring life to your emotions, either positively or negatively. When you intend to be kind and care for others, you act with kind deeds, openness, and acceptance. When you intend to get more of what you want without care for others, you may act kindly, however, your actions will be mixed with manipulation, inauthenticity, and possibly ill will. When a person is unclear about their intention, they cause havoc, confusion, and pain and their Gracious Quotient falls. It is very important to monitor your intentions because they will lead to either higher levels of graciousness or, the more difficult lower levels. When you monitor your intention, be honest and notice how often your thoughts hold pure or impure intentions. The purpose of this practice is not to open the door to judgment but rather a place to begin noticing pureness, intentions, and improvements needed.

To increase your graciousness, you may want to think about this more concretely. Perhaps increasing your graciousness is that of the flow of a mountain river. The Gracious Quotient can rise or fall within seconds throughout the day. Just like a river, graciousness elevates swiftly when the water level is high and may also trickle slowly when the water level is low. The foundation of your graciousness relies on your full openness at any moment.

Fueled by Emotions

The Current is fueled by and delivered through our emotions. Emotions are associated with feelings, behaviors, and thoughts that send out Currents that others can pick up on. Emotions are a natural reaction triggered by a wide range of internal and external factors, such as thoughts, memories, physical sensations, and social interactions. Emotions are brought to life through your intentions which, in turn, elicit a response to others or a situation and are connected to what we have become attuned to from past experiences. Emotions alert you to your surroundings or what is happening to you.

To align with what we choose to send out, we need to be sovereign and clear on the Current we are sending out.

Many of us lose our sovereignty when our emotions lead us to pleasing others or feeling threatened and therefore start to lose a sense of ourselves. When this happens, we become nebulous (i.e., unclear or hazy), allowing others to control, influence, and pull us into transmitting their Current instead of our own. We have all been there when other people's guidance conflicts with the knowing in our souls.

The first step is to be aware that at any given moment, you will feel various Currents, some of which are not your own but will influence emotions. The next step is acknowledging that the emotion is driven by thoughts and intentions associated with the Current. When you don't acknowledge the underlying Current, chaos can result. Being nebulous and being in chaos is due to a lack of sovereignty and an inability to understand the emotion. This leads to the overwhelming feeling that it is just a "bad day" and everything is "happening to you." It doesn't have to be this way. You have a choice. You can choose whether to stay in this "bad day" or to move into higher levels of graciousness by managing emotions and the Current.

Emotional responses are a valuable tool to guide you in understanding your attunement in a situation but is not a defining statement about who you are.

There are four main types of Currents, moving from pure love—the kind that takes your breath away—to the least pure type of ill-will and wishing harm. Each type is associated with an emotion and impacts you and others. Being conscious is defined as an individual's ability to perceive their environment, thoughts, feelings, and emotions and their ability to process information, make decisions, and construct appropriate responses to each type of Current.

Type One: Pure Love

This type of Current has a low density and high graciousness feel. When we or others send out a pure love Current, that current makes us feel welcomed, loved, and cherished. It is the perfect unison of the soul and the Divine, an unconditional love that takes your breath away as the intensity of this unison removes your humanness, bringing you into experiencing a miraculous connection. This intensity is so strong that the human body and mind cannot sustain it for long.

Pure Love is a gift. You cannot achieve this; the Divine offers it when you are most receptive. Your soul will recognize this moment as pure love and can purify anything, any issue, and potential ailments. Once we feel this type of Current, you will likely strive to return to it throughout your life. This Current is experienced as pure love, pure acceptance, pure intentions, and pure blessings.

Type Two: Love

The love Current has a low to moderate density and a high to mid-level of graciousness feeling. When we or others send out a Current of love, we feel welcomed, however, may start to experience some judgment. This Current has a feel of experiencing love, loving more naturally and with an ease of acceptance. That said, the Current can also bring a sense of conditions around this love since in our humanness, we do sometimes set conditions on love. We may feel abundance and a sense of connection. There may still exist remnants of conditional love, but the love you feel and express elicits happier and more settled emotions. You feel a sense of enlightened excitement to share your soul's blessing and be open to others sharing theirs. This Current surrounds us with a sweetness that invites others to unwind and release their worries.

If the Current becomes more dense, it may feel like there are more conditions to adhere to. We may feel like our love for others is only delivered "if" a specific condition is met. For example, there may be various tests that must be passed by you or others as a constant monitoring system to see if you are living up to these conditions. You may say, "I love you, but if you do this, I'm not going to love you as much." or "I'll still love you, but it's going to be less." When there are high conditions around love, the Current shifts toward a nebulous Current. This Current becomes more dense with the energy of disappointment, exhaustion and becomes unwelcoming. Even though this Current is filled with love, it can create confusion, and mixed messaging and leave us overwhelmed with uncertainty.

Type Three: Nebulous

The third type of Current is one of a nebulous nature, is of moderate to high density and is found in lower levels of graciousness. In this Current, we sense mixed messages, a feeling of confusion and being unwelcome. We can feel exhaustion with ourselves and the outside world and where nothing seems to matter when we touch upon this Current. As we become immersed in this Current, we feel intense confusion, and the stories we begin to tell ourselves illicit feelings of inadequacy and revenge. Individuals may feel depressed with an underlying sense that there is, or must be, a better way.

When in this Current, you know there is still good around you, within you, and within others, and although you are not confused about this, you are so depleted and exhausted that you start to move into a space of numbness, a state where you may see beauty, but not feel it. This is a transitory state where it is easy to move out of this Current and just as easy to stay in it and allow yourself to embrace exhaustion and confusion. The Current can become more dense, leading to a distorted view. This Current is sending out an alert to others to stay away, yet, the "rescuers" of humankind will respond to this Current and work hard to save others even if it looks nearly impossible.

As this Current becomes denser, confusion escalates leaving us to feel victimized with a desire to blame others for our pain. This Current is strong and hard to see through. When you are in this Current, you lose your sense of self and are unsure what to hang onto to avoid confusion. This Current of high density entices you to move into the fourth type of Current called Ill-Will. That said, to stay in graciousness, and thus the freedom to be yourself, you must be aware of this Current and focus on your newfound knowledge of your soul and move away from this type of Current.

Type Four: Ill-Will

The Current of ill-will is one of high density and low levels of graciousness. This Current makes us feel destructive, have high anxiety and fear, and have a sense of ill will towards others. This is the darkest Current and when, you get near it, you can become overwhelmed and absorbed into feelings of hatred, deceitfulness, and ill-will. It may show up as a strong feeling or desire to control others and to have others do your bidding without respect or regard for the individual. Those around you will sense your Current and be compelled to stay away as they sense your desire to destroy.

When we feel the Current of ill-will (and we all occasionally do), understand that this Current is attractive to darker currents. Ill-will is created to harm others, our earth, and our authentic selves. Be cautious when you sense an ill-will Current as graciousness does not exist here and you can easily be drafted into this Current. If you are the one sending this Current of ill-will, ask your soul to forgive you for the ill-will you bring and work to repair any damage that you have done to yourself and others.

To avoid falling into the ill-will Current, you must first recognize you are in a nebulous Current. Therefore, you may choose not to commiserate with others about your exhaustion as this will only amplify the nebulous Current and start moving you into the ill-will Current. Try to move toward your soul and focus on allowing yourself to become less dense. This will help move you quickly toward a Current of love.

Practice: Regulate your Current

The following practice will help you create awareness and consistency to emit the Current of love.

1. For three weeks, take three days each week to practice this exercise at least three times a day and at least three hours apart.

2. On those days, set a reminder to pause and be come aware of which zone you are in at that time.

3. If you are not sending out the Current of love, try to find ways to shift into that Current. Notice how long you can stay in the Current. Check again in a few hours, and repeat.

4. Notice how this practice works for you. Are you able to start recognizing which zone you fall within the most? Are you able to see how being in a specific Current affects you? Are you able to be come aware of how shifting to other Currents allows you more acceptance of yourself and your blessings?

Week	Day	Hour	Current	Good? / Need to change?	How did you make the shift?
1	1	10 a.m.	Nebulous	I need to shift to the current of love.	I sat quietly and asked the current to shift, and it did.
1	1	1 p.m.	Love	I stayed in the current of love.	I was invited to lunch and happily accepted, enjoying the company.
1	1	6 p.m.	Nebulous	I need to shift to the current of love.	I took the time to recognize my current and those around me. I recognized the need for sovereignty and shifting to a better current. I then did so.

In Summary

Managing your Current is one method to help you raise your Gracious Quotient. The four types of Current are identified as a means to help you clarify and understand what Current you are sending out most of the day. Your goal may be to be in the Current of Love most of the time and to create the space that allows you to fulfill your life's purpose, live in a freer state without all the world's worries, and encourage others to do the same.

Your Gracious Shell remains solid from birth, and the space outside of it, ebbs and flows with the world around us and with how we choose to both influence and be influenced. Perhaps using an analogy can help you associate the Current concept and will keep it in the forefront of your mind. A river that flows freely and swiftly is the love Current and carries with it all of our blessings. A river with lower levels of water, flowing slowly, (nebulous Current) reminds us to pay attention to the slowing of the flow as our minds start to fill with judgment and conditions that must be met before we trust or allow our blessings to come through. As the river slows further, and the rocks and plants become more prominent, exhaustion enters as the water struggles to find its path. There may be very little flow at this point. If not replenished, our minds take over, and we devise stories of our own accord to make us feel better. The river's flow has become so stagnant and there is no opportunity for your soul to come through, causing your Current to move into ill-will, and it can be challenging to look inward to see why events are happening around you and to you.

Increasing your Gracious Quotient requires a deep understanding of your Current, like the high levels in the river versus a nearly dry riverbed with no flow, so that you can manage your Current and keep the channels open for your soul to easily flow into the world.

CHAPTER SEVEN

Managing Attunement:
Emotions, Beliefs and Core Values

Your soul contains your knowing, essence, and pulse. Both your soul and the outside of the Gracious Shell create a meaningful story for others while the Gracious Shell is the space between them. The combination of your soul's essence, knowing and pulse, with your human side, is called your "personality." To show all of you, to be the best you, you must have more of your soul transmitting outward through the Gracious Shell while keeping the current you emit low in density and high in graciousness. Suppressing your soul, consciously or unconsciously, is typically done from what you are attuned to. Unfortunately, if you are unaware of your soul and of what you are attuned to, you will present yourself as a reflection of others, not your true self. This leads to a disconnection to yourself, with inner conflict, dissatisfaction, and lack of authenticity. While we respect the social norms we live with, we can find that graciousness elevates our true nature fostering personal growth, deep connections, and a real appreciation for what we are here to do.

Outside the Gracious Shell is your human side, inside the Gracious Shell is your soul. Your attunement, physical presence, emotions, and mind are outside the Gracious Shell. To understand where your attunement comes from and how to manage the attunement, we begin by understanding emotions, emotional density, beliefs, and core values.

Understanding Emotions

The first concept to understand is that of emotions. Emotions are associated with feelings, behaviors, and thoughts that send out currents, which, others can pick up on. Emotions are a natural reaction triggered by a wide range of factors, such as thoughts, memories, physical sensations, and social interactions. Emotions are brought to life through your intentions which, in turn, create your response in a situation and is connected to what we have become attuned to from past experiences. An emotion alerts you to your surroundings and what is happening.

When emotions become more overwhelming, we call this high density, meaning you may not be able to see others or a situation clearly.

As many say, "emotions are energy in motion" or otherwise "e...motion" that is outside your Gracious Shell and is an excellent reminder that emotions do not represent who you are. Emotions are merely a current coming from you or coming from others around you. You may give ownership to these emotions by saying things such as: "I am angry" or "I am in love." Instead, it is more accurate to say, "I *feel* angry" or "I *feel* love." This allows you to remain sovereign and is a reminder that you are not your emotions. Emotions can tell you a story that represents what you want to believe. We tend to stay with that to which we are attuned, what we believe, and our values instead of acknowledging that the emotion is not a story—it is just that, an emotion.

It is common to see joy and pleasure as bringing light and love while sadness, depression, and despair as bringing darkness and a sense of hopelessness. But it is essential to understand that these emotions have the same energetic force and can create a call for hope, peace, love, or revenge. Why, then, do some emotions elicit a "positive" response while others elicit a "negative" response?

This is simply because emotions go hand in hand with your intentions, what you seek to evoke or create.

> *Emotions are not who you are;*
> *they express your intentions.*

As a child, emotions are seemingly in charge because their ego is in survival mode. A child is dependent on the guidance of others, the nurturing of others, and the provision of safety, food, and shelter. As you grow older, you realize that the emotions you experience can be managed instead of allowing them to dictate your day.

As an adult, emotions are signals of what you have become attuned to and hold within your belief system (except for biochemical issues within the body). What you are typically aware of is your own response to a situation, how it makes you feel, and perhaps the unpleasant reality of your responses. You may seek to understand why a particular response occurred. You may start to feel less than or better than others because of emotional responses. It is common to use emotional responses as a judgment on how healthy a person is based on our own definition of "healthy," "right," or "wrong."

Some believe that emotions, reveal who we are. For example, if you cry a lot, you may be labeled as "weak," "emotional" or "empathetic." Or, if you anger easily, you may be seen as a "hot head" or "irrational." This is simply not the case. You are not an emotion.

Graciousness requires you to forego judging others and accept that they are who they are. What graciousness offers you is the ability to acknowledge emotions, where they come from, and how to transform them for higher graciousness. Graciousness helps you understand that emotions are part of a larger system that flows from your intentions, belief strands, and core values. One way to think about this is shown in the following diagram.

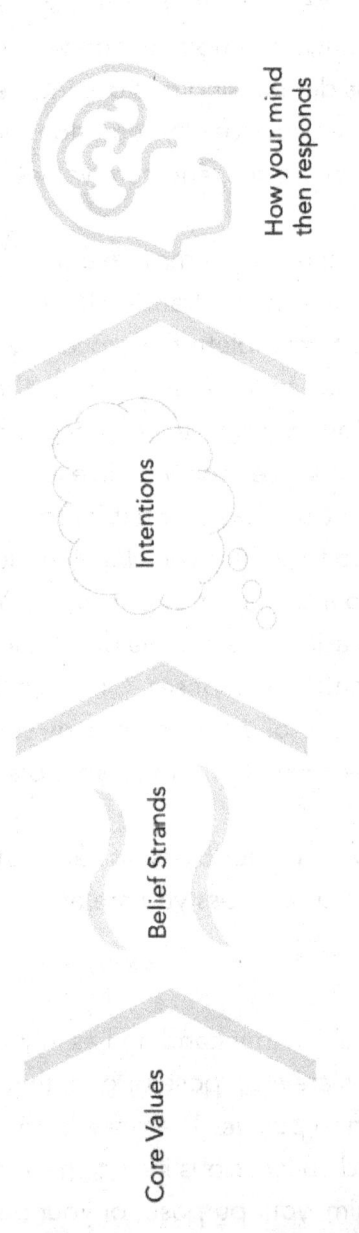

Core Values → Belief Strands → Intentions → How your mind then responds

When a situation arises, your mind may behave in a way you didn't expect, and the emotions become active. At this point, your mind takes over and responds based on your intentions. These intentions are years in the making and were formed by your belief strands. Each belief strand is based on one or more of your core values developed early in life.

Your core values are the foundation of this system. As you increase your Gracious Quotient, you will start to slow down and consider pausing or stopping before responding so you can consider the emotions you elicited, intentions, belief strands, and core values.

Understanding your core values may take time initially as you walk through the belief strands. However, eventually, you'll be able to complete the process quickly as you become attuned to it. When you walk through the belief strands, you may start to see images of the past, experience your senses coming alive and enter into a deeper thought process on what happened or what you are attuned to so that you clearly understand the foundation of your beliefs and core values. You may then decide to adjust the core values, beliefs, intention, emotions, and/or responses. Or, you may find that your responses are solid and the energy you put into your response is sovereign with all your blessings.

The key is to attune to your blessings at whatever level of graciousness you are at.

Intentions

The first concept in this understanding lies in your intentions. Intentions are a purpose or goal that one has explicitly chosen to pursue. There are both conscious intentions and unconscious intentions. Intention is your hope, your aim, your purpose, or your desire to satisfy a need you have. An unconscious intention is a mindset that you have not explicitly chosen or a motivational structure that you're unaware of but that nonetheless influences your thoughts and behavior.

If your intention is satisfied, you may feel positive, neutral, or nothing at all, which is how many of us feel, at least for part of the day. If your intention isn't satisfied, then you may feel negative emotions. Let's look at some examples of intentions and values and how they may show up.

Joe has a core value of independence, while Hannah has a core value of helping others. When Hannah opens a door for Joe, Joe immediately responds with irritation. Hannah is confused as she feels she is being kind! Joe and Hannah's experience is the same: feeling undervalued, humiliated, and insulted, yet neither means to hurt the other. Joe had underlying intentions that in any situation, he would open doors himself or feel worthless. Hannah's underlying intentions were to show kindness which would illustrate her worthiness. Both had an intention, whether conscious or unconscious, and they did not get the response from each other that they believed matched their intentions. Their intentions and each other's response elicited responses and ultimately created a negative current. This obstructed their true blessings that would have sent a current of gracious acceptance and appreciation.

Liz was chatting with her friend and mentioned that everyone around her says she is "too emotional" and cannot be trusted to manage important situations. They discussed it and discovered that Liz's intentions to be seen, honored, and revered were not being met. Liz then realized that as a child, her parents tended not to see her or acknowledge her needs and wants. Her mother was overwhelmed and had no room to support her children emotionally. This led Liz to create the belief that when going into any situation of authority, she was not valuable or seen. This belief led to daily emotional hurricanes, and others became confused and bewildered. Liz came to understand that she was never delighted or satisfied. Liz slowly started to see that she was seen and honored in some situations and that her intention had to be reworked. She tested a new intention: I am seen, honored, and heard. As she began talking with co-workers and discussing projects, she found that her new intention made her feel more balanced in her approach to situations and to others. Thus, she became focused on honest, high-integrity intentions before she went into meetings.

Emotions can be erratic. Most of us experience many emotions throughout the day, which may not drive our responses significantly. It is when these emotions have a higher density and become charged (or intensified) that we may respond in ways that are not in alignment with our soul. When we feel emotions that drive us to respond, it is best to take a moment and consider our intentions and then determine how best to respond. This flow from intentions to responses is one that we can understand and manage. As we become more skilled interpreters of the emotions we feel, we can interpret what is happening and respond in a gracious way.

Emotional Density

The second concept to consider after intention is emotional density. Once you understand that emotions don't define you, you can be objective and witness emotions instead of being defined by them. You can see the emotions as messages. If you are not objective, you may notice the emotions intensify, which is called emotional density. When emotions are heightened (either positive or negative), and your thoughts take over your mind, the density becomes thick, like a fog you cannot see through. As a result, your self-awareness diminishes, as does your sovereignty.

Imagine that the space around your physical body is open, gracious, and inviting. Imagine your soul is a space of three feet around your body in all directions, like a bubble and the Gracious Shell sits on the outer rim of the soul. Sitting immediately outside the Gracious Shell is your humanness, with all the attunements, physical representation and currents.

Try to remember a time when you felt anger. The outside perimeter of the Gracious Shell then becomes dense and thickened.

The growing density of emotions could have been expressed as "I am so angry." The current you then sent out became more dense, and there was less room for you to experience openness and graciousness, and your freedom dissipated.

As emotions become dense, the pivotal moment occurs when you enter the "all about me" state. Here, you are fueling your ego and emotions and moving toward a lower level of graciousness. A state of high-density emotion means there is no room for anything other than that emotion—not another person, not your soul—just the emotion. The same experience can happen in the case of the emotion of elation, where the emotion becomes dense. There is now less room for you to experience openness, graciousness, and your freedom dissipates. The spectrum of emotions, from elation to anger, is ego-driven, and you lose the ability to be sovereign, therefore not being able to fulfill your life's purpose. To be clear, we are all human and will experience a range of emotions.

You have a choice in each moment to focus on graciousness instead of your ego.

By knowing emotion as outside of the Gracious Shell, you may think, "I sense the current of anger around me." At this moment, you can choose to witness the emotion and begin to identify the intention that isn't being met. For example: "I sense anger around me because I had intended that a very personal story would not be shared with others." You can then choose to respond to your friend, "I have lost faith and trust in you as you committed to not sharing a very personal story with others." This way, you don't hold on to emotions and increase the density. You release the emotions, therefore, you don't carry this to the next situation and do not contribute to this negative situation.

When several emotions arise, and you do not release those emotions, it creates an "emotional bundle." The density of the emotional bundle can be immediately recognized as the extreme intensity of the emotions. Extremely intense emotions mean that the emotion has become very dense and seeks to gain more of your focus while pulling your focus away from your soul. This will take more and more energy and power away from you and your blessings. As the emotion becomes more dense, your Gracious Quotient lowers. The lower levels of graciousness will intensify the harm you bring to yourself and others. And, as you move away from your ability to share your blessings, you start moving toward being nebulous, into despair, and possibly into ill-will. How can you quickly shift out of this momentum and diffuse the situation?

Remember, emotions drive humans more than anything else. Emotions are a result of your attunement to your core values, beliefs and are an expression of your intentions. At the same time, emotions do not have to define you as a person as long as you remember to see emotions as energetic currents outside your Gracious Shell. You can witness the emotion and what it is trying to tell you and reduce the density of that emotion. How you respond is one hundred percent under your direction.

Practice: Guiding Your Emotions

This simple practice can guide you when you have a strong emotional response to a situation. Note: If you are emotional due to a crime that has occurred, facing abuse, or are in a dire situation, please contact those who can help and assist you. Otherwise, for daily and less impactful emotions, recognize that you can stop and use the P.A.D. principle. P.A.D. stands for "Pause. Ask. Do."

1. **Pause**—Grab a pen and paper. Write down the name of the strong emotion that you are feeling. (i.e., Sadness). Now imagine pushing the emotion outside of your body—outside of your mind. See the emotion as an energetic current outside of you

and become curious about the emotion—not your response to it. Remind yourself that while you are experiencing the emotion, it does not define you. Be careful not to bring more energy to the emotion by discussing it with others.

2. **Ask**—Ask the emotion(s) questions such as: Why are you here? What do you want? Emotion, what can you teach me so that I can bring your current into the world for good and not destruction? Engage the emotion: "Show me what you want me to see." This may take you several attempts.

3. **Do**—Write your learnings down in a journal, on sticky notes, or in some other visible form so you can return to it when the emotional current has shifted to a more gracious quality. It could take minutes or hours as the emotion keeps finding its way back in. Be patient with yourself and the emotion(s).

You now have a sense of intentions and their ability to elicit dense emotions. Where do your intentions originate from? Your intentions are directly related to your core values and beliefs.

Core Values

The third concept to consider is core values. Your core values were gathered from what you learned and adopted as a child. Core values are concepts that most people are familiar with; however, when another is asked to share their core values, the question may leave them speechless. What words should you use? Core values can be seen in everything you think, feel, and do. You already have them. However, discovering exactly what they are takes time, honesty, and perseverance.

A core value is something you cherish the most; it guides your every move. It is the basic, most fundamental principle you live by and are guided by.

Core values are very personal. We might use the following words to define them: authentic, trustworthy, integrity, humility, independence, loving, kind, abundance, family, accountability, perseverance, discipline, etc. There are literally hundreds of words you can choose to define your core values. As you take the time and begin to list your core values, you may even have conflicting core values. It is important to do your best to try and list as many as you can to determine which conflict and which support each other.

Practice: Identify Core Values

A simple exercise to identify your core values is to write them out.

1. Get a pack of sticky notes and on each sticky note, add your core value one word at a time. You may be able to name ten or fifty—it doesn't matter, just do your best.

2. Once you've written as many as you can, choose a way to organize your thoughts, and start to organize your stickies so that you can clearly see what your primary core values are, and what your secondary core values are.

A **primary core value** threads through everything you do in life. A **secondary core value** is one that you use most of the time but not always. For example, if core values are individualism, dignity, respect, family is everything, achievements, equal rights, perseverance, authenticity, sacrifice, caring, sharing, scarcity, and abundance, then some primary core values will roll up secondary core values underneath it and could include family is everything which would hold sacrifice, caring, and sharing; individualism would hold respect, dignity, achievement, equal rights, perseverance, and authenticity. This example shows how core values can be in conflict. The conflict is with family is everything vs. individualism and scarcity vs abundance.

Belief Strands

The fourth concept to consider is the belief strands and how they begin to form. You can have multiple belief strands that stem from one core value, and there may be belief strands that form from a combination of core values.

In the diagram below, an individual has identified their core values as scarcity, abundance, and independence. They became attuned to these core values as a child and started to form belief strands, which then led to their intentions. Their intentions are based on what they came to expect and how they respond when their expectations are met or not met. In the example, they are being asked to financially support another who can work and care for themselves. In this case, the core values form deeply embedded belief strands that guide their intentions. Then, when their intentions are unmet, a response is elicited that may or may not align with their soul.

Intentions

My intention is that I am honored for what I do and honor others for what they do. I will take care of myself, love others deeply, share of myself, and honor myself. I will keep for myself what I worked hard for and others can keep for themselves what they work hard for.

Belief Strands

- I will do what it takes to have financial abundance.

- I will give of myself to show others how abundance of love feels.

- I will make sure I am safe, protected, and firm with my boundaries.

Core Values
- Scarcity
- Abundance
- Independence

Until you are aware of your intention, it isn't easy to modify your response to a situation or know how your soul can guide you into higher levels of graciousness. Someone can experience high-density emotions to the point where their reaction is at a very low level of graciousness. For example: when driving and someone pulls in front of you, you may be inclined to escalate to frustration or anger. Your emotional response to this situation is defined by a sequence of core values, belief strands and intentions. If your core value is respect, your belief strand may be kindness and understanding, and your intentions may be that people should treat you well. In this traffic situation, your emotions became intensified, and your response was anger.

Until now, you have been trained to respond in a particular way. As you practice, you will gain a full understanding of how you have been trained. From there, the ability to see your soul, the Gracious Shell and your human side enhances your ability to see others the same way, thereby setting you free from all that entraps you. Your intentions will become pure, your beliefs will be for the highest good, and you will raise your Gracious Quotient. The goal is to have the current you send out transmitting in a balanced way that frees you and others. By attuning your core values, beliefs, and intentions to a higher level of graciousness, you can more quickly be able to get to sovereignty, release your ego and acknowledge your discomfort with the disregard you feel from another, and release the emotion.

While you accept the person for who they are, you may still find their actions to be unacceptable.

In Summary

When you feel uncomfortable with your response, consider how your core values, belief strands, and intentions played a role in your response. It may take some time to be clear and authentic in your review of how your core values, beliefs, and intentions played a part in your discomfort. When you are ready, take some time to work through the discovery process and then consider how you would like to revise your process. Ask yourself, would you like to revise your core values, beliefs, and intentions?

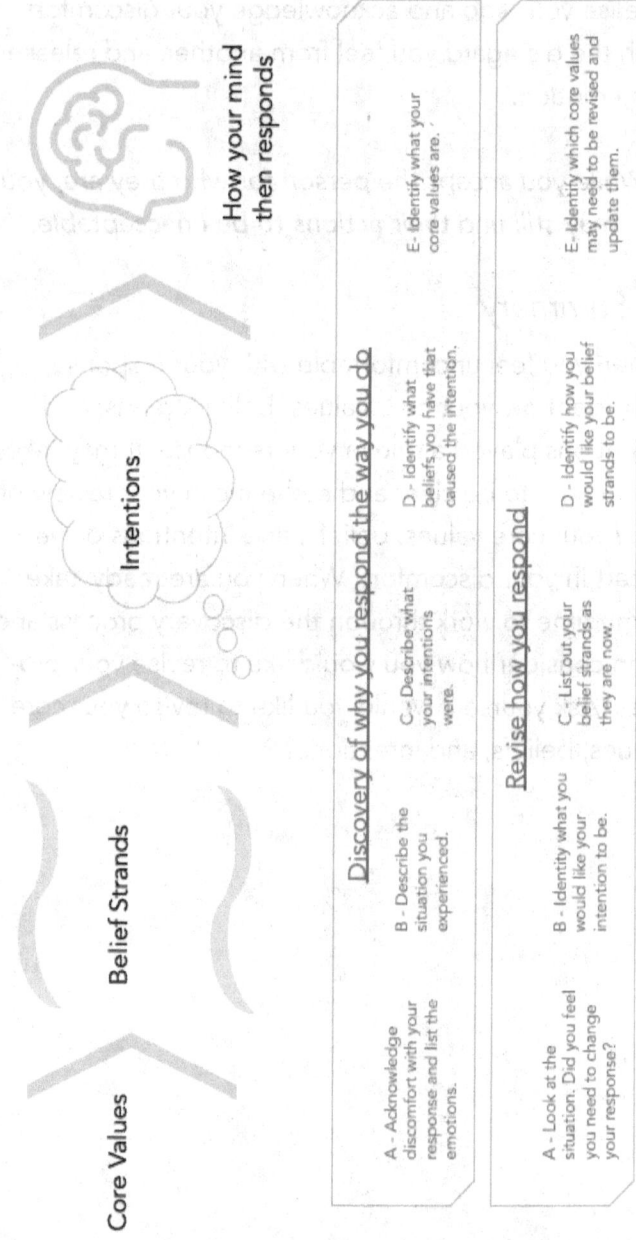

Core Values → Belief Strands → Intentions → How your mind then responds

Discovery of why you respond the way you do

A - Acknowledge discomfort with your response and list the emotions.

B - Describe the situation you experienced.

C - Describe what your intentions were.

D - Identify what beliefs you have that caused the intention.

E - Identify what your core values are.

Revise how you respond

A - Look at the situation. Did you feel you need to change your response?

B - Identify what you would like your intention to be.

C - List out your belief strands as they are now.

D - Identify how you would like your belief strands to be.

E - Identify which core values may need to be revised and update them.

CHAPTER EIGHT
Creation and Actualization

Gracious creation refers to creating an environment that supports what you want to actualize. Creation is delivered by your soul. Creation differs based on which level of graciousness you are in. In higher levels of graciousness, creation is an amazing opportunity to bring forth a gracious current that allows you and others to actualize what you desire. Creating is setting up the environment, the current, that must be in place before you fully and sustainably actualize. To create graciously, consider what level of graciousness you are in and try to be at the highest level possible, acknowledge the type of current you are emitting and shift to the a more gracious current if needed, and finally commit to accommodate and appreciate this creation.

Actualizing, referring to fulfilling one's potential or becoming the best version of oneself, how you will be in the creation requires being open to the fullness and richness of what you want. It involves self-awareness, personal growth, and the commitment to focus on reaching one's goals. Creation is a concept already used by many parents, trainers, athletes, spiritual leaders, and inventors with incredible results. Actualization requires sovereignty, dedication, perseverance, and, most importantly, a strong connection to your soul.

Your soul offers the undeniable knowing that your soul will both guide you and support you.

To Begin

The key is to be attuned to your soul as creation and actualization comes from the soul. To create and actualize what you need and what matters most, you must understand what level of graciousness you are in and what level you need be in to secure creating and actualizing. There are three concepts summarized below to consider before you create and actualize:

1. **Graciousness Level:** What level of graciousness are you in? There is a significant difference in what gets created and actualized based on your current level of graciousness. If you create from a gracious level 4, you will create and actualize from a highly judgmental state resulting in more of the same. You will not be creating or actualizing from your soul; you will be creating and actualizing more from outside influences. In level 3, ownership is important, meaning you will likely focus on actualizing ownership. You may want a reward for all your hard work.

Meanwhile, being in your highest level of graciousness, you will choose a reward that allows your essence to show up in all that you do and allows your soul to work through you. Not all of us can be in the highest levels of graciousness, which is okay. However, it is where you likely have the highest level of pure reward, peace, and acknowledgment of knowing you are creating and being the best version of yourself. Many of us want to actualize a job, a home, an individual, a feeling, a better body, or status. We cannot create and actualize meaningful and fulfilling abundance when our level of graciousness is low.

2. **Current:** If you send out a strong current at a high level of graciousness, you will actualize at that level. Always identify your current and determine if your ability to create will actualize what you really want. The nebulous current and ill will current only result in actualizing a portion of what you desire, and often, you will create in the wrong direction. This results in disappointment, as the fullness and richness of what you truly want to actualize is lost.

3. **Space:** Consider if there is space in your life for what you actualize. Will you truly have the ability to manage what you want to create? For example, if you create a welcoming and inviting environment for a romantic partner to be attracted to, can you sustain that environment? In addition, you will actualize who you are within that environment. Can you genuinely honor that person and make room for that individual to be a part of your life? Can you hold space for what that person brings with them? How will those additions impact your self-actualization?

To become more familiar with the three concepts above, let's look at an example:

Mark achieved a gracious level 7 with the love current before he began creating. He envisioned the creation as an environment of abundance, freedom, and safety. His goal was to actualize buying a car so that he could get a higher paying job, help his mom get medical treatment, and have the freedom to pick up his date. He worked hard to save funds and even took on extra jobs. He was so close to the amount he needed and only had another week before the car was sold to another buyer. As exhaustion set in, he began moving into the Nebulous current and feeling desperate. He was able to notice this and caught himself.

In an attempt to move out of this current, Mark went to the seller of the car and explained why he needed the car, and the seller explained why he had a due date. Mark offered the seller all the funds he had accumulated and asked for another month to pay the remaining amount.

The seller appreciated the creation (unbeknownst to the seller) and the authenticity of Mark's current and noticed a trustworthy individual. Mark then offered the seller a precious item to hold onto for the month as collateral for the remaining funds. Mark paid the car off in the month ahead. Mark actualized this from a gracious level 7. When he felt his current moving down into the nebulous current, he immediately acted and moved his current into the love current. He learned that while his brain could only take him so far, he needed to focus on his soul, the creation, and the energy to actualize the car.

Once you consider the three concepts of gracious level, current, and space, you will want to ensure that your soul flows through. While it may be challenging initially, graciousness will come through more effortlessly over time. The brain typically guides your body and life, and that is critical to understand. With the Gracious Quotient, this paradigm shifts to your soul guiding your choices.

As discussed, graciousness requires that you look at where you are and what you can do to move to the highest level of graciousness before you create and actualize. The soul isn't something you can operate on, touch, or see in a mirror. Most people usually want to hear an intuitive whisper or message. They listen and seek the same level of conversation they might have with others, yet this isn't what typically is found. When listening to your soul, sit still and write down what immediately enters your mind without dissecting it. This will help you "hear" better. If you allow words or images to come to you and start processing them through your mind, you will lose trust that you are getting intuitive whispers or messages. You will also miss the true meaning of the messages.

Eliza is in gracious level 8 and wants to create a space to receive visions. The creation she is asking her soul to provide is a current of openness, acceptance, focus, and of ethereal nature. To actualize, she set aside an hour to sit in meditation. She went into a room, closed the door, dimmed the lights, opened the windows for fresh air, and began to allow herself to just sit and be with her soul. She noticed her eyes wandered around the room and started thinking about her life.

As she moved to focus on nothing but her breath, she began drifting into a feeling of openness, of sensing without her ears and eyes and without all her normal thoughts. She then allowed her imagination to flow in a new, unique way. She envisioned herself moving into an open, ethereal space without boundaries. She stayed with this for some time and allowed her imagination to take in the sensations she was experiencing of peace, acceptance, and Divine consciousness she was experiencing. These brought forth a sensation in her chest as she saw a yellow daisy forming and coming into a clear shape with seven petals and a dark center. She got the sense that she was the center of the flower, and each of the petals represented her life choices.

When she began to rouse from meditation and out of the vision, she wrote: "I am the center of my own flower, what petals am I choosing to grow, and how shall I nourish them to bring the greatest beauty to this world?" She then began to spend time with the concept, identifying what she felt each of the seven petals represented, and then developed her plan on how to give each petal what it needed to thrive and flourish. Through this, she actualized her soul's purpose of bringing beauty to the world.

Starting to Actualize

How do you start to actualize? First, create an environment in which your actualization can thrive. Start small, perhaps like Eliza, creating the environment and envisioning a beautiful flower. Once you accomplish the beautiful flower, you may be ready to consider another actualization within the environment you asked your soul to create. You will need to be authentic about what level of graciousness you are in when you want to create and actualize. Specifically, choose being in the highest level of graciousness. Ensure you understand that level, what it feels like, what it requires, and what it looks like. Most people want abundance. So as with the plant, you give it what it needs, and you hold the created space around so it can grow. The creation of space is open, free, pure energetic space that allows you to fully connect to the Divine, to your soul, and to what you want to actualize.

143

In Summary

Many of us read books, listen to lectures, and focus on what we most desire. If we should focus on being in higher levels of graciousness, then why do those in lower levels of graciousness sometimes receive abundance of possessions? These individuals do not live a gracious life, however, we all can actualize from a place of low graciousness, nebulous or ill-will currents, and be attuned to possession is power. The current we send out is the current we get back. In the lower levels of graciousness, you will not fulfill your soul's purpose nor have the ability to offer the world what is rightfully yours to give—your blessings. You will continually get more of the same. Therefore, an individual in higher levels of graciousness, can receive an abundance of possessions, fulfill their soul's purpose, and deliver their blessings. This individual is receiving the current they emit.

CHAPTER NINE
Daily Practice

Daily practices arise from a very personal desire to be more gracious and are a way to establish a routine and structure in your life to consciously raise your level of graciousness. These practices can provide a sense of meaning and purpose as they will help you to stay more connected to your soul. With higher levels of graciousness comes a more profound sense of freedom, a high level of sovereignty, and a knowing deep in your soul that you fully accept yourself. As you become more self-aware, you'll see emotions, such as disappointment, anger, frustration, love, joy, and tenderness, as just emotions.

Emotions are messengers that help us learn more about the current around us.

Below we offer three ten-minute and three one-hour practices. Choose a time that works with your schedule. Preparing a space for your daily practice can help create a conducive environment to support your connection to your soul.

◊ Choose a quiet, comfortable space free from distractions and without interruptions.

◊ Add elements that support calmness and relaxation, such as soft lighting, natural elements like plants, bells, chimes, or soft music.

To begin, create a way to acknowledge the start of the practice, such as a bell, chime, hum, or song. There are many ways to start; however, sounds seem to be the best way to get all the senses into awareness, which is why this method is so often used and recommended. During and at the end of each practice, you are guided to sip water. Sipping water stimulates your mind and body, offering an awareness of what you just learned. Upon completion, you will be guided to finish sipping the water, which will help you prepare for the rest of your day.

Practice One: Ten Minutes (Identify your Essence before starting this practice)

1. Have ready: Timer, pen, paper, and a glass of water.

2. On your paper, create three equal columns with the headers: "Essence," "For Good," and "Impact."

3. Set the timer for ten minutes and then acknowledge the start of the practice.

4. One minute—Write your essence, when completed, pause and sip the water.

5. Five minutes—Write a few sentences on how your essence showed up for the good of yourself and/or others. When complete, sip the water.

6. Three minutes—Write one sentence on the impact of your essence. When complete, finish drinking the water.

7. Acknowledge the end of the practice.

Then at the beginning and end of each day, refresh your memory on the writings you created for at least seven days.

Example of Ten-minute Essence Practice

Essence	For the Good	Impact
My Essence is one of a bridge builder where I support those and guide them on their path to reach their goals.	A young woman wanted to find a job that best suited her. We spent an hour discussing what mattered to her, her values, and what kind of job would be rewarding. She was tasked with looking at companies, and I was tasked with finding contacts. We came back together to identify where a good fit may exist based on her views, her values, and my contacts. I contacted those who could help her secure interviews with key companies.	Walking with her showed her a path she would not have considered before due to her level of experience and confidence. She was gracious in accepting help and followed through with the interviews. I walked her over the bridge of knowing how to get interviews with companies that matched her values instead of any companies where her values would not be appreciated.

Practice Two: Ten Minutes (Current)

1. Have ready: Timer and glass of water

2. Set the timer for ten minutes—acknowledge the start of the practice.

3. Intentionally walk into an imagined or real circle with your arms raised outward and up to the comfort level you can manage.

4. Close your eyes and breathe in and out sincerely three to four times while your arms are still raised.

5. Keep your eyes closed, and imagine a multitude of colors swirling around you but not in you, and once you have identified those colors convert them into the four energetic currents: true love, love, nebulous, and ill-will. All the currents will not be the same size in force. It could be one current is larger than the others.

6. Start with the current of ill-will. Imagine keeping this current outside your body, tell the current it is time to convert to a better current, and imagine it moving into the nebulous current. Now you will have two colors/currents. Then, when you feel secure, move into the Love current. Allow your imagination to release all the worries, emotions, and thoughts, and watch as they leave your space and mind.

7. Move your body slowly and bask in the love current. As you near the end of the practice, invite the love current to be ever present and become the largest current for your day.

8. Complete the practice by sipping a glass of water.

Refer to this imagery throughout the day, especially when you are not emitting from the current of love or feel drawn to the currents of nebulous or ill-will.

Practice: Ten Minutes (Intention—Use P.A.D)

1. Have ready: Timer, Pen, Paper, and glass of water.

2. On your paper, create three equal columns with the headers: Pause. Ask. Do.

3. Set the timer for ten minutes—Acknowledge the start of the practice.

4. Three minutes—Pause and consider your intention during an emotional event, positive or negative. Write the intention down in the first column. When completed, pause and sip the water.

5. Five minutes—Ask your soul how you can change or honor the intention you had. Write this in the second column. When complete, pause and sip the

water.

6. Two minutes—Do—Write a power sentence in the third column that comes from a place of sovereignty and personal power where your intention is pure. When completed, finish the water.

7. Acknowledge the end of the practice. At the beginning and end of each day, refresh your memory on the writings you created for at least seven days.

Example of Ten-minute Intention Practice

Pause—Intention	Ask—Change intention or honor intention	Do - Write a Power Sentence
My friend missed yet another lunch with me, leaving me to sit alone at a restaurant. I was humiliated and ashamed. I believed her yet again and felt abandoned as I thought that this time she would honor our commitment. My Intention was that my friend would see my pain and care enough to offer respect and acknowledgment that my time is equally important!	As I sit with my soul searching not for protection but for the truth. I hear that I just gave my power to others, that I was not being sovereign. I was a victim in this situation and offered my friend the role of making me feel less than. I have the power to acknowledge that my friend has difficulties keeping her commitments, and I have the power to act accordingly and spend time with those who honor our time together.	I will stay in my power and sovereignty by releasing control over others. I understand the consequence of not being sovereign, as it causes chaos and pain to me and those around me.

152

The hour-long practices are designed to help you resolve more profound issues. You will want to try these when you have the time, ability to focus, when you are alone and are willing to be honest and open with yourself.

Practice: One Hour (My Soul)

A more extended practice requires more consideration and planning. You must find a space to focus entirely on your soul. This means planning to eliminate outside noises and influences, such as people talking or cars going by, which can bring you back into the awareness of the outside world. It is best if you have white noise, either using a headset or something else that can prevent you from hearing other noises. The mind has a habit of deciding that if it hears a noise, it will move its attention in that direction. The mind needs to be still, or it will interfere with the ability to go inside to your soul.

1. You might like to begin with some quiet meditation to allow your soul to start showing up, or just sit comfortably and focus on your breath. Within a few minutes, imagery and words will likely flow in. Allow all the imagery to be present and invite it to show up. It does not come with your goals; it comes with its own agenda and messages. Become part of the imagery and allow it to transform itself.

2. Recognize that this isn't from the outside world but the inside world. You are tuning out all external influences and focusing on hearing only the soul which is quiet, calm, and peaceful. Do not allow your mind to determine what it is you hear. It may be simple things such as "I feel my breath expanding" or "I feel my entire body relaxing." And as all that happens, imagine all the space between your self and the outside world expands. As this expands, you will gain a sense of peace, of freedom from all that is outside. This space is your sacred space, your soul.

3. Keep releasing any thought that keeps entering your mind; let it flow away like passing clouds or a leaf floating down a stream.

4. Now go deeper. Imagine yourself in a glorious, crystal-clear body of water. Feel the ever-so-slight coolness of this water as it touches your skin. Imagine your entire body floating as the water wraps around every inch of your body.

This is your first practice of opening up to your soul. There is no requirement to write, sip water, or examine anything as it just supports you to become attuned to your soul.

Practice Two—One Hour
(Current and Sovereignty)

The first step is to refresh your understanding of the four currents.

1. Find a quiet and private space to concentrate and have a journal, pen or pencil available.

2. Think about your day and determine what current you were in during the morning, afternoon, and evening.

3. For each current, identify whether you were sovereign (the only current you can be sovereign in is that of love) and the impact you had on yourself and others. If you are sovereign, you likely have a positive impact. If you were not sovereign, you likely brought chaos into the situation. Become aware of your sovereignty, or lack thereof, and the impact of your actions.

This way, you can chart your experiences and start to manage your current and sovereignty to become more gracious.

Time of Day	Current (True Love, Love, Nebulous, Ill Will)	Sovereign?	Impact
Morning	Love current	Yes	Peace, consistency, openness, and generosity
Afternoon	Ill Will	No	Anger, mistakes at work, others were frustrated with me, I snapped verbally at a client (creating chaos)
Evening	Nebulous	No	Sad, wished I could be different, confused about why I did what I did, high guilt, and started to understand I needed to apologize.

Practice Three —One Hour (Belief Strands)

Belief strands are the key to understanding your emotional response to situations. Emotional responses don't represent who you are—they represent what you are attuned to, either by choice or training. When you understand your soul, become sovereign, and are in higher levels of graciousness, you can choose your true core values and belief strands. Below is a practice that will help you assess a situation and determine what is essential for you to acknowledge and possibly update.

Discover Step A: Spend ten to twenty minutes acknowledging your discomfort from an emotional response to a situation. Did you respond overzealously or poorly? Did you tell yourself, "This is not really me," or "I am better than this!" Write down as many emotions/sensations that you experienced.

Discover Step B: Define the situation. In twenty minutes, try to define the situation you identified above with as much detail as possible. In that time, focus only on the facts, with little emotion, response, or excuse. Leave judgment out of it. Think about the loop your thoughts are often in, and be objective as possible. Choose only one situation, a moment in time, an event, and answer the following questions:

1. Who was involved, or what was involved?

2. Is there a history attached to it? If so, can you leave that behind, or is it truly relevant?

3. What rules and roles were present at this moment? Include your response to the situation, and ask yourself: What did I do? Be honest. At that moment, did you notice your voice change, tone, or volume?

4. What was your outward behavior? Your body language?

5. Were you able to hear the other(s) or listen? Were you seeking to be "right" or "win"?

6. Were the emotions positive or negative?

7. Did it throw you off center?

8. Did you have the impulse to act?

Discover Step C: Define your intention in five to ten–minutes. Intentions may be unconscious, so take your time to really sift through the experience and define what you believed was going to happen, what you intended to accomplish, and what expectation(s) you had in that situation. If, for example, you believe we all deserve to be heard, then your intention may have been that you will be heard no matter what. Again, think about this factually, leaving out all emotion and removing all judgment. What did you intend to have happen?

Discover Step D: Take the intention(s) identified above and ask yourself, what were your beliefs in that situation? Spend five to ten minutes composing your belief strand. A belief strand is a single sentence such as "I believe everyone has a voice worthy of hearing." or "I believe that only powerful voices are heard."

Discover Step E: Spend two to three minutes answering the question, what is the core value that this belief strand stems from? It may be "Equality" or "We all matter."

Then begin revising. Decide if you wish to change a core value. Decide if your belief strand is essential to keep or needs to be updated. Then re-write your intention so that it can be met in most situations. Then try it out! If it works—great! When trying it out, keep reminding yourself of your new way of being. If it does not work, rework the steps above until you find the core values, beliefs, and intentions that bring peace to you.

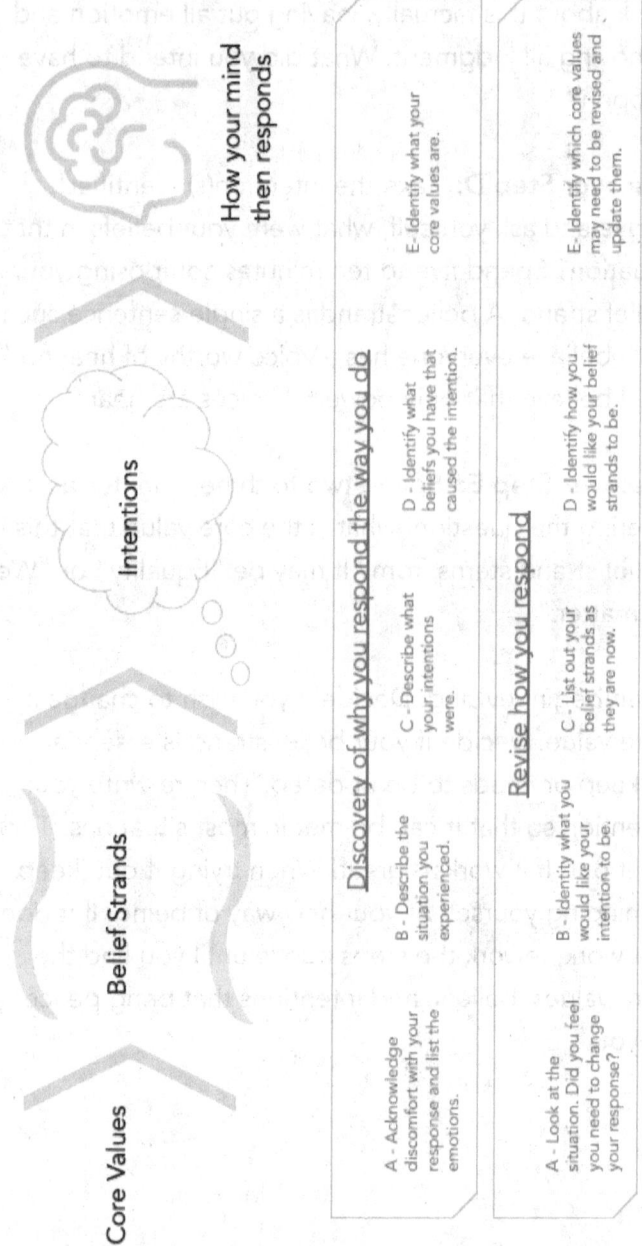

Core Values

Belief Strands

Intentions

How your mind then responds

Discovery of why you respond the way you do

A - Acknowledge discomfort with your response and list the emotions.

B - Describe the situation you experienced.

C - Describe what your intentions were.

D - Identify what beliefs you have that caused the intention.

E- Identify what your core values are.

Revise how you respond

A - Look at the situation. Did you feel you need to change your response?

B - Identity what you would like your intention to be.

C - List out your belief strands as they are now.

D - Identify how you would like your belief strands to be.

E- Identify which core values may need to be revised and update them.

Practice: Using Mantras

Mantras, for this purpose, are statements said aloud in repetition to give greater space to your soul. By opening up space, you are opening up space for the Divine. By opening space, you become freer to release all that holds you back from living your most authentic and gracious life.

This practice is best done after you have completed a few belief-strand practices. Belief strands will help you find a path to your soul, one filled with graciousness. The more conscious you become, the more you can release others from your judgment, opening up more space for your soul. Why? So, you are free to be yourself, create the life your soul guides you to, and have the peace needed to fulfill your soul's purpose.

A mantra can be a reminder to strengthen whatever you are already doing, what you may need to change, or what to appreciate more. The key is creating a mantra in your soul's best interest. How can you know what is in your soul's best interest if you are just beginning? First, do the soul practice, and secondly, complete the belief strands practice. There can be hundreds of belief strands, and it can feel overwhelming to decide where to start. To make this all manageable, focus on three at a time. Then, try filling out the following grid, or create your own list of needs using the grid for reference.

What would you like to strengthen?	What needs to change?	Create a Mantra
Allow the truth of the situation to present itself, uninhibited by a story you created	A belief strand that the other shoe will always drop/something bad always happens.	Listen with an open heart and without judgment.
(1)	(2)	(3)

For each of the three statements, start to identify the following: your belief, how you got this belief, and your soul's truth. Then write this down and place it where it best serves you as a reminder.

For example, in the grid to the left, under "What needs to change?" Jason wrote the following: "Looking for the other shoe to drop." Based on Jason's belief strands, it meant that things didn't typically go well most of the time, and feelings got hurt. This was learned in childhood from school. It may stay with Jason all the time and in every situation. The belief has been that "no matter what, something will go wrong." The change in belief here could be more aligned with the idea that there is a balance between what goes right and wrong, and the focus can be on the balance.

Next, write the mantra on a colorful sticky notes and place them somewhere visible that you will see them every day, such as on the bathroom mirror, by the coffee pot, or on your computer. The end mantra is "Listen with an open heart and without judgment."

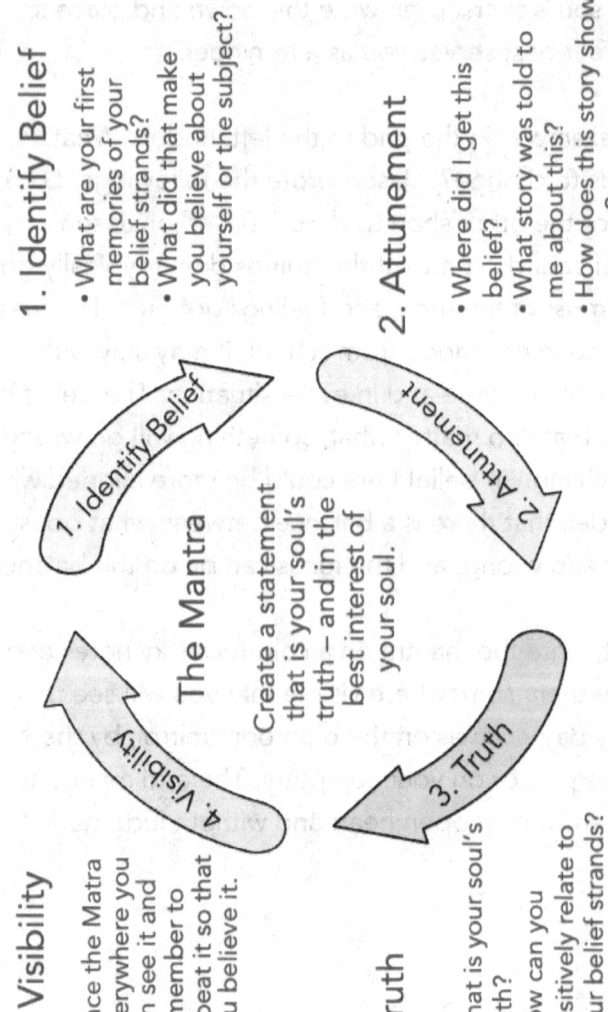

1. Identify Belief

- What are your first memories of your belief strands?
- What did that make you believe about yourself or the subject?

2. Attunement

- Where did I get this belief?
- What story was told to me about this?
- How does this story show up now?

The Mantra

Create a statement that is your soul's truth – and in the best interest of your soul.

3. Truth

- What is your soul's truth?
- How can you positively relate to your belief strands?

4. Visibility

Place the Matra everywhere you can see it and remember to repeat it so that you believe it.

In Summary

Being sovereign in your soul, or within, requires a conscious effort to be aware of yourself and how you interfere with both your soul and your blessings. The above practices are general and are meant to offer ideas on how a practice can look. You can design your own practice(s) anytime you choose. Get curious and experiment with the practices and ways that help you connect with your soul. Your connection is uniquely yours and can only happen if you feel comfortable with the way it is happening. This is ultimately why so many people feel unable to connect with their soul because they work hard to connect in a way that works for others, not themselves. So, choose your own way.

©2023 Gracious Quotient ®. All rights reserved.

CHAPTER TEN
The Moment of Choice

Freedom comes in each choice you make if you are sovereign, are in the current of love, and are in higher levels of graciousness, level 7 or above. Some choices may come with little to no consequence, while others may have significant consequences. It is possible that you do not feel able to make such consequential choices, which leads to a need for time, advice, and reflection before deciding. While those may still be essential when making consequential choices, it is critical to be free of others' influence in the moment of choice, because you and you alone will live with the consequences, good or bad, of your choices. Others may try to influence you to avoid being impacted by your choice, but is that gracious? In the moment of choice, what matters most is that you are at your highest level of graciousness, whether that is a level 6 or even a 9, it is whichever level you consistently achieve.

The moment of choice brings to the forefront what you have been attuned to thus far. Only you can agree to who you are now. Many of us have faced trauma and are attuned to our parent's way or our community's way, and we have core values, beliefs, and intentions that drive what we see, how we see it, and how we respond. These attunements then come out in a current that is in alignment with our level of graciousness at any given moment and affects our blessings, both to ourselves and to others. Therefore, what we receive from being aware of all these attunements at the moment we make a choice can be in the best interest of our soul, which is ultimately for the best interest of ourselves and others. Remember that some of our past will stay attached to us, much like a vine growing around a tree. Some parts of the vine can be easily removed, while others have become embedded in the bark. The tree forms around the vine. And it just is; therefore, during a moment of choice, you will want to consider if the embedded vine impacts the opportunity to make a strong choice. If it is, seek your highest level of graciousness and allow your soul to guide you.

Facing Each Moment

The moment of choice occurs constantly. To be in a higher level of graciousness requires facing each moment of choice with a keen attunement to our soul. If we feel tugged by our ego, have a dense current, and are impacted by others' currents, our attunement to our soul wanes, and we face the moment of choice with less purity, sovereignty, and benefit. On the flip side, if we are attuned to our soul, not only can we face moments of choice with purity, sovereignty, and higher benefit, but we can also bring forth our blessings.

A simple process to help you with moments of choice is to place reminders throughout your home or work-space. These reminders include ribbons in your favorite color, pictures that capture what you feel in your highest level of graciousness, soothing scents, calming music, or words and sayings that help you attune to your soul.

Another process to take you deeper and provide a stronger attunement to your soul is releasing the cords that bind you. Cords are an attachment to another person's energy and flow both ways. This cording impacts your ability to see clearly during a moment of choice. Therefore, it is in everyone's best interest to release it. It is like they are always with you and always in your mind. Releasing these cords will offer you more sovereignty and graciousness during a moment of choice. You simply consider the person who you feel has the most influence on you and visualize a cord from you to them. Visualize the healing of the cord and wounds from the cord. Then visualize releasing the cord.

It is vital that in your moment of choice, you are making choices that are in the best interest of your soul, not your ego, and not for others or for limiting beliefs. We all get caught up in the current of the world, and we feed off this force with the expectation that it will guide us however, this is not the influence required to bring out our unique blessings. The Gracious Quotient is a reminder of all that you are here for, all the many blessings you are to bring to yourself and to others.

Much of the positive impact you can bring into this world is based on your soul, and much of the negative impact you bring is outside the shell.

Bringing higher levels of graciousness into your world will reward you with a freedom that you are unique all unto yourself, that you have many blessings to offer that take your breath away, and that each person is here to bring exactly what is required at just the right moment.

Remember, each moment of choice is yours and yours alone. We wish you the very best and send you a pure, low-density, current to remind you how exciting it is to see your soul shine. We send beautiful blessings to you and all those around you.

CITATIONS
Footnotes

1. See definition for sovereignty pg. 18

2. See definition for attunement pg. 9

3. American Psychological Association. (n.d.) Compassion. In APA dictionary of psychology. Retrieved September, 2022 from https://dictionary.apa.org/compassion

4. Mayo Clinic. (n.d.) Mindfulness. Retrieved September, 2022 from https://www.mayoclinic.org/healthy-lifestyle/consumer-health/in-depth/mindfulness-exercises/art-20046356#:~:text=Mindfulness%20is%20a%20type%20of,mind%20and%20help%20reduce%20stress.

5. Mindful. (n.d.) Mindfulness. Retrieved September, 2022 from https://www.mindful.org/what-is-mindfulness/

6. Andrea L. Bell, LCSW, SEP (June 19, 2018) Somatic Mindfulness: What Is My Body Telling Me? (And Should I Listen?) Retrieved from https://www.goodtherapy.org/blog/somatic-mindfulness-what-is-my-body-telling-me-and-should-i-listen-0619185

7. Merriam-Webster. (n.d.) Culture. Retrieved September, 2022 from https://www.merriam-webster.com/dictionary/culture